TIWI STORY

MAVIS KERINAIUA is a Tiwi historian, educator and researcher. She has contributed to historical exhibits at the Northern Territory Library and the Patakijiyali Museum and worked as a researcher for the Australian National University and Flinders University. She has worked in cultural liaison for the Department of the Prime Minister and Cabinet and in education on Bathurst Island. Creator of the Turtuni Framework for research practice, Kerinaiua is an expert in culturally responsive and appropriate research.

LAURA RADEMAKER is a historian of Aboriginal Australia and religion with a PhD from the Australian National University and an interest in oral history. She is the author of *Found in Translation* (University of Hawai'i), shortlisted for the NSW Premier's Australian History Prize and awarded the Australian Historical Association's Hancock Prize. She is also co-author with Traditional Owners of *Bible in Buffalo Country*, winner of the NT Chief Minister's Award for History. She has written for *ABC Religion and Ethics* and *The Conversation* and appeared on ABC Radio National.

'*Tiwi Story* is a powerful collection of pieces written by Tiwi people about their experiences of colonisation. Their recounts are an important telling of past and present issues confronting Tiwi people and their culture, shining a necessary spotlight on a history of forced assimilation and suppression of Indigenous culture and language. This book is a testament to the strength of the Tiwi people and provides insight into the ongoing impact of colonisation on Indigenous cultures.'

TERRI JANKE

TIWI STORY

TURNING HISTORY DOWNSIDE UP

MAVIS KERINAIUA AND LAURA RADEMAKER

NEWSOUTH

UNSW Press acknowledges the Bedegal people, the Traditional Owners of the unceded territory on which the Randwick and Kensington campuses of UNSW are situated, and recognises their continuing connection to Country and culture. We pay our respects to their Elders past and present.

A NewSouth book

Published by
NewSouth Publishing
University of New South Wales Press Ltd
University of New South Wales
Sydney NSW 2052
AUSTRALIA
https://unsw.press/

A catalogue record for this book is available from the National Library of Australia

ISBN   9781742238128 (paperback)
        9781742238807 (ebook)
        9781742239743 (ePDF)

Internal design Josephine Pajor-Markus
Cover design Jenna Lee
Cover artwork Purrukuparli ngirramini by Harold Porkilari. © Harold Porkilari.
    Photograph courtesy of NGV
Printer Griffin Press

All reasonable efforts were taken to obtain permission to use copyright material reproduced in this book, but in some cases copyright could not be traced. The authors welcome information in this regard.

This book is printed on paper using fibre supplied from plantation or sustainably managed forests.

This book is dedicated to all Tiwi people,
past and present.

This book contains names and images of people who have passed away. We do so with permission of the Tiwi people. This book contains quotations from historical sources that contain offensive language and ideas. These do not reflect our views but the views of people at the time.

CONTENTS

History is for our kids' future. It's for kids to know what happened in the past. And we need kids to know what happened to this place … Otherwise we lose everything if we don't have an older person telling stories what happened in the past. They should talk about their culture and keep it strong for the next generation to come. Otherwise, it will fade away.

— Magdalen Kelantumama

CONTRIBUTORS

Calista Kantilla

Calista Kantilla is a Tiwi elder and knowledge-holder. Calista is the oldest living Tiwi woman today and holds important knowledge of Tiwi experience and culture. Calista sings in the Strong Women's group and has toured her music all across Australia.

Romolo Kantilla

Romolo Kantilla is an emerging Tiwi leader. Romolo is proud to share Tiwi history and culture with those visiting the islands and has worked in Tiwi tourism teaching visitors his culture and history for numerous years. He also has a background as a talented footy player, having played for the Tapalinga Superstars.

Magdalen Kelantumama

Magdalen Kelantumama is a Tiwi linguist, educator and respected elder. She was a leader in the Tiwi bilingual school program and now contributes to cultural heritage work at the Patakijiyali Museum.

Dulcie Kelantumama

The late Dulcie Kelantumama was a respected Tiwi elder and knowledge-holder. For many years, Dulcie worked as a teacher. Dulcie sang in the Strong Women's group, famed for touring Australia and for its cross-cultural musical collaborations.

Teddy Portaminni

Teddy Portaminni is a Tiwi elder who worked as a schoolteacher for many years. He is founder and owner of Tarntipi Bush Camp, training visitors to the Tiwi Islands in cross-cultural awareness and Tiwi culture. Teddy also sits on the Tiwi Land Council.

Barry Puruntatameri

The late Barry Puruntatameri was an important Tiwi leader. Throughout his career, Barry served on the Tiwi Islands Regional Council as Deputy Mayor and also as President of Nguiu (now Wurrumiyanga) Council. Barry also served on the Tiwi Health Board, a community-controlled health service, and the Tiwi Education Board, the governing body for the Tiwi-owned and -operated Tiwi College.

Pirrawayingi Marius Puruntatameri

Pirrawayingi Puruntatameri is presently Lord Mayor of the Tiwi Islands Regional Council, and sits on the Board of Tiwi College and of Nungalinya College in Darwin. He has also served as chair of the Northern Territory Elders Visiting Program, supporting incarcerated First Nations people.

1

HISTORY IS HEALING

Mavis Kerinaiua

I believe history is for healing. But you need to tell the whole story, the good and the bad. Telling the truth to the younger ones, the next generation, will make them strong. We want them to be proud of their identity and to be strong.

Did you know some of the earliest European history of Australia happened on the Tiwi Islands? So Tiwi history must also be part of reconciliation. It's a healing process. It's time to acknowledge what happened and to help each other understand. That's why we've written this book.

I come from Wurrumiyanga, 80 kilometres from the coast of Darwin, Northern Territory. My family land group is Mantiyupwi, we are the traditional owners of Wurrumiyanga. My kinship and relations are the Jilarruwi, the Brolga Tribe. My totem dance is Tatuwali: shark.

We Tiwi people want to care for our Country and hold onto our cultural values. And our history comes into that, which is why it is important. We want to showcase our histories, especially the good side. These are stories of adaptation, survival and independence. And we want to honour the Old People and help each family group to share their stories, to collect and collate all these stories from all the Tiwi families. This is to empower them too and acknowledge their past and what they've done for the Tiwi Islands.

History is also important for Tiwi to have that sense of where we belong and where we come from. Because it hasn't been that long since the Catholic priest Father Gsell came here and started the first mission at Nguiu (now Wurrumiyanga). It wasn't that long ago: 1911. My grandmother, Mabel Wulungura, was one of those girls who went to the dormitory. They were known as the bush girls.

So it's good to tell the story from the Mission days up to the days of Tiwi independence. I was only a child when self-determination started. My late father, Alan Kerinaiua, played a big part towards self-determination. In 1971 he and our forefathers founded the Nguiu Ullintjinni Association shop and started talking about their own land council. Later, in 1978, the Tiwi men broke away from the Northern Land Council and formed their own Tiwi Land Council. It's good to capture those moments so that the young ones can have an understanding of the trials and tribulations of becoming proud, independent Tiwi people.

Tiwi young people don't have the opportunity to learn or hear stories about their history in schools or at home. In the modern days, young people no longer practise most of the ancient rituals and ceremony. They're not learning all the old songs. So having role models is especially important. This is why I've been working alongside historian Laura Rademaker as co-author of this book. It's good to share history for kids, because hopefully one day they will become historians or researchers too and write about their people.

We have a lot of Tiwi people here today that are still strong in faith. So we acknowledge the church too for some of the work they did here in terms of educating our people. But it's also a painful story. It was hard in those days with the policies they had then, and policies are always changing. But it's important to also bring out the good points from that time. The church did eventually relinquish its position in terms of running the community. It handed over the schools and the clinic to Tiwi people themselves. The mission was the first administrators, but they passed that back, they gave it back to the Tiwi. Good things came out of that handover; the school

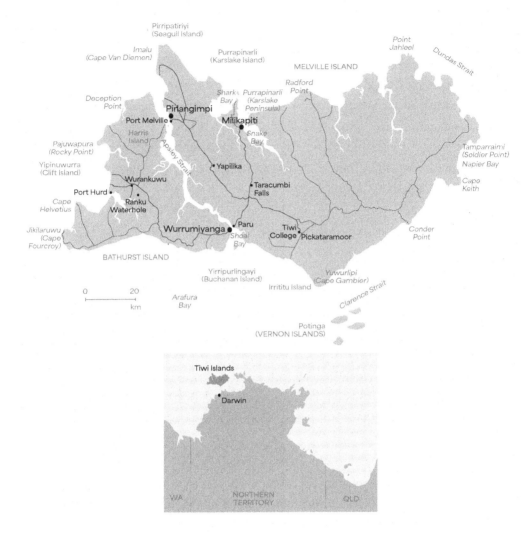

Map of the Tiwi Islands (with permission of the Tiwi Land Council).

had Tiwi principals. But that wasn't continued, today the principals are non-Tiwi people. That's why it's important to strengthen Tiwi governance so we can carry on running our own programs.

Now we are dealing with a lot of community disturbance, through gambling, drugs and alcohol, and domestic violence, all the anti-social behaviour. We want to show our young ones that the Old People have been through that too, but they had more self-awareness,

3

they were mindful of themselves and others. I want to reinstate that confidence which brings that clarity. The Old People, they knew who they were. But our young ones today sometimes feel inadequate and lost in today's modern world. When history comes it builds up that confidence again and that sense of belonging and knowing. It empowers people, especially young ones, and I believe it creates more heroes too. They will want to be part of it, the legacy that the Old People have left behind.

I'm not the first Tiwi person to write history. Some Tiwi histories are written down in books, others are in songs. They're still sung today, especially for funeral ceremonies. In the past, my aunty Beatrice Kerinaiua, a linguist and writer, did some work with the school and the Mission. She wrote down histories and traditional stories about Tiwi people. I grew up watching my aunty and cousins, and my other late sister, Leah, working on the bilingual education program. As a child, I helped with the picture books for the literacy centre, because the bilingual program was strong in those days. We told our history through language and through the translation work. So my aunties knew and spoke about history and it was written the way they spoke it.

The difference now is that I come in with research experience and university training. I've done a lot of professional writing and reporting. But I still understand the feelings, the emotions of the story and of the people. So, I can write that side too. It means I can interpret the Tiwi stories in a western context.

The western way of doing research that Laura uses is slightly different to our Tiwi way of researching. This is where I come in, bringing this new way of doing research from the ground up as a Tiwi woman. My impression is that the western research principles just don't quite understand how important relationships are. That's the beautiful thing about Tiwi, and other Indigenous people. That's where we're different. For us, research goes much, much deeper because of the connections, the relationships.

Recently, I've been developing what we call the Turtuni Framework. It's a Tiwi narrative that explains what Tiwi want – our cultural protocols – for those who want to work with us. It's a guideline when researching on the Tiwi Islands. It's putting Tiwi in charge in the decision-making. It's all about collaboration, partnership, and agreement. We want to make sure that Tiwi traditional beliefs, knowledge and values will always be strong, adaptable, but more so alive, especially through caring for Country initiatives and working with researchers. Whatever work we do, we also want young people to be part of it, whether through employment, in land management or in science, or as researchers. And there's also another side to it about accepting our past, the Ancestors. And we need to build on that foundation from the past, the Old People.

I enjoyed working with Laura. I bumped into her when she was with the Australian Catholic University. I got to know her more because I have an interest in history. I thought this is a really good way for me to start getting involved with historians and with researchers. I wanted to join her because I think I can bring a lot into it as a cultural broker and historian, especially in terms of promoting Tiwi history and collecting histories from families.

The biggest threat Tiwi are facing today is climate change. I am worried about it, for our bush food, our plants and animals – which is where we get our song and dance and identity – and for coastal erosion and sink holes. The high sea level rise is already happening, and we are seeing changes now. We are worried about our Tiwi bush food, and Country, especially burial sites. If we lose our bush resources there won't be enough food, because the bush and sea are our supermarket, that's where we get our food. The high sea level is rising right in front of our heritage areas, where the old mission church and the convent, old school and renal clinic are.

This is where climate adaptation will come in handy. And this is where history comes in handy too. It's why it's important for Tiwi to understand history, because it was climate change that separated us from mainland, the high sea level rise over those thousands of years. We have to adapt to it. The important part is climate adaptation.

In our mythology we have our legend Murtankala. She's a woman creator, who created the Tiwi Nation. Back in those days there were no land, no sea, no trees. Most people lived underground, so she rose from the underground with three children, carrying them in her basket. She was looking for a place to put her children. And at that time, as she crawled out, water came rushing up behind her. She formed the Tiwi Islands as she travelled. Before she disappeared, she filled the place, put plants and animals on their Country, and got the sun goddess to hold the torch to light and warm the children.

The story tells us about how climate change came, and high sea level rises, and how we walked over from mainland. You have your Tiwi perspective on how we were separated from the world alongside the one from science. We've seen climate change before, and we adapted. So, it's very important to understand how climate change does play a part in how things change, land, and our culture changes too. But it's also important to have the young ones appreciate the past, what happened too. All our warriors are heroes, our leaders that created this beautiful community for us. The beautiful thing about Tiwi culture is there's room for the future to always adapt.

2

TURNING AROUND

Laura Rademaker

A polygamous priest first introduced me to Tiwi history. According to his account, he was quite the enthusiast for women; he had 150 'wives'.

Wurrumiyanga (formerly 'Nguiu') is now a small town on the Tiwi Islands, just off the coast of Darwin in the Northern Territory of Australia. But it began as a Catholic mission in 1911. That self-styled polygamous priest (and eventually bishop), Francis Xavier Gsell, recounted the story of building the mission there through the 'purchase' of girls in his 1954 memoir, *The Bishop with 150 Wives*, published in French, German and English.

According to Gsell's account, when he first set up camp on the islands, Tiwi people ignored him. Some men would come and go, constructing the mission in return for rations, but no women. In Tiwi custom, girls were promised before birth to their future husbands. At puberty, they married men who might already have numerous wives. To Gsell, this was slavery – women were a Tiwi man's 'chattels, his slaves, and merely part of his movable possessions'. A mission to a people steeped in this tradition was doomed to fail. Little girls would come into the mission to the care of nuns but, when the day for their marriage came, he wrote, 'some old chap would emerge from the forest to claim her as prey. With tears in her eyes, she would leave us'.[1]

That was apparently until one girl, who he named Martina, refused to go with her promised husband and sought refuge at the

7

mission. Gsell dated the incident to 1921, though archival records indicate it was earlier, probably around 1916.[2] 'An ugly mob of muttering gesticulating tribesmen' supposedly rallied at the mission gates. Martina clung to the priest. Gsell prayed. The idea came to him: 'I will buy Martina from these men'. He laid out his possessions on a table: a blanket, flour, tobacco, a knife and hatchet, steel, a mirror, a teapot, calico, tinned meat and treacle. The men saw the display, their eyes 'gleaming' with desire:

'All is yours to take away with you but, in return, you must let me have the girl you have come for'.

The men conferred in low whispers, grunting, 'we sell the girl'.

So Martina remained at the mission and, according to Gsell, grew up into a 'good and devoted Christian – a gentle, sweet and charitable soul'.

She was the first of many; 'one hundred and fifty little girls followed the same bizarre process', according to his story.[3] The girls were baptised and became Catholics and the mission began to see its first successes in Christianising the Tiwi people. Tiwi women were supposedly freed from an oppressive kinship system to marry whom they chose. The mission was established on the buying of wives, according to the missionary priest.

There are some problems with Gsell's account. You may have bristled at its stereotypes of Aboriginal men as violent and abusive. Or perhaps you found its depiction of vulnerable Aboriginal women cringeworthy. Maybe you winced at the bizarre attitude to sexuality from a supposedly celibate priest (did I mention they dressed the dormitory girls in skirts, and nothing else? Gsell's contemporaries certainly noticed). All that is there.

But its main problem is that it is not the story Tiwi people tell about their history. That is why this book exists.

This Catholic mission to the Tiwi was part of a renewed push

Gsell and his 'wives', dressed for First Communion.
MSC Archives, Kensington

in the early 20th century on the part of Australian governments and churches to 'protect', 'Christianise' and 'civilise' Aboriginal people in remote parts of Australia who had, so far, lived largely without Europeans intruding in their daily lives. Gsell was a priest of the Missionaries of the Sacred Heart (*Missionnaires du Sacré-Coeur* or 'MSCs'), an order of priests dedicated to spreading the Catholic faith in all places. The MSCs worked together with nuns (the Daughters of Our Lady of the Sacred Heart or 'OLSH') to evangelise the Tiwi as well as provide western education and medical care. At the mission, girls stayed in the dormitory under the care of nuns. Their families camped on the beach nearby, working for missionaries in return for rations.

Today, there are three main towns on the islands: Wurrumiyanga on Bathurst Island (the former mission), Pirlangimpi on Melville Island (formerly Garden Point Mission) and Milikapiti (formerly

Snake Bay Aboriginal Settlement). Nowadays, the Tiwi are famous in Australia for art, sport and film. Their art is recognised for its Pukumani poles – ceremonial grave posts, carved and painted with unique, intricate designs – and its batik-style fabric art. Australian Rules Football dominates Tiwi social life. Players from the islands are well represented in the professional game; the great footy families, the Kantillas, Riolis, Longs, Tipungwutis, McDonalds (and more) are Tiwi. The Tiwi have also made their mark in Australian cinematic history. Tiwi man Robert Tudawali starred in the landmark 1955 film *Jedda*, the first Australian colour feature film. Their Country featured in the recent *Top End Wedding* as an idyllic island home and before that, they were the backdrop for Baz Luhrmann's *Australia*. The Tiwi Islands have a special place in the Australian collective consciousness as a Top End paradise.

But before the Tiwi were known for artistic and sporting prowess and beautiful tropical vistas, they were known for the mission. The 150 wives story shocks. It was meant to, although it shocks now for different reasons than those Gsell envisaged. He thought his description was playful. A tease. A priest a trafficker in slave girls? Ridiculous! Now it seems sinister. In the aftermath of revelations of abuse in religious institutions around the globe – there has been a lengthy and involved Royal Commission in Australia – a story about a priest and his girl 'wives' can no longer be read for fun. This is also part of the Tiwi story.

Given this, you might expect the Tiwi to want nothing to do with the Catholic Church or the mission. You might expect Tiwi to feel shame at their history. I did. So I was startled when I went to the Tiwi Islands and met women who grew up in the mission dormitory, daughters and granddaughters of the so-called 150 'wives'. These women were proudly Catholic and proudly Tiwi. Far from shame at the 150 wives story, they view these girls – the 150 – as founders of their community. They were pioneers. So how could the Tiwi view their history this way?

Turning histories around

For so long, the story of Australia's First Nations people has been told mainly as one of destruction, victimhood and suffering. It is a pretty depressing history. Especially so because this is not the only story First Nations people have to tell. As many Aboriginal Australians know, their forebears were strong. So this book is about telling a better story.

Based on oral histories with Tiwi people, Mavis Kerinaiua and I want to re-write that negative narrative of Australia's Aboriginal history. In this book, Tiwi people's own testimonies come first, with the colonial archival record of only secondary importance. Without downplaying the trauma of colonisation, we want to draw out the stories of survival, hope and even humour, that are also part of First Nations experiences. We are convinced that telling history in this way is healing, both for the Tiwi community but also for the Australian nation as it begins to come to terms with its past. We hope this book might answer back to Gsell a century later, and share other sides of the story, drawing attention to the voices of Tiwi, especially Tiwi women, their culture, their faith, their community, their history. Our message is that, in those days, the Old People were strong.

Tiwi people have plenty to be proud of. This little tropical island community has more than its fair share of surprising stories that turn ideas of Australian history upside down. This book is also about unexpected twists and turns. Tiwi history is full of inversions – things turning upside down or topsy-turvy – and conversions: turning around, changing direction. Aboriginal history is often about space, place and travels more than it is about time, dates and chronology. Thinking about twists and turns, how people were oriented to each other, grounds this story in relationships between people on Country rather than events or dates.

And the 150 wives story is one of the world turned upside down. Gsell's version features many hallmarks associated with imperial and missionary narratives of white men's dealings with Indigenous peoples. Gsell presented himself as someone who could successfully cross the boundaries of black and white, 'civilised' and 'savage', Catholic and pagan, only to draw Tiwi people into 'civilised' Catholic living. He drew on familiar ideas about 'going troppo', 'going native' and 'jungle fever' to make himself into a virtuous saviour figure of Indigenous women. Gsell was not actually the first bishop to 'go native'. In South Africa, Anglican Bishop John William Colenso was ridiculed by his peers in the 1850s and 1860s for the concessions he made for Indigenous cultures around polygamy. He suggested that, in some cultural contexts, perhaps polygamy was okay. Colenso was famously said to have been 'converted' by the Zulu, becoming the butt of racist jokes.[4] But not Gsell. His story of 'going native' on polygamy functioned to neutralise any white fears that these boundaries might be blurred. Gsell's actions were a pantomime. He meant to win the Tiwi and change their society from within.

White people's fascination with 'going native' has a long history. At the beginning of the 20th century, popular imagination had it that the white man who 'went native' was perhaps marooned on a tropical island. He cast off 'civilised' manners and adopted local customs, often marrying Indigenous women. But by doing so, he reinforces, instead of disrupts, racial hierarchies. Gsell's ability to take on the role of polygamist functioned to prove the supposed superiority of his society and religion to those of the Tiwi. Gsell's telling revelled in transgressing boundaries of 'civilised' and 'savage', as these inversions confirmed to his readers his strength of character, and ultimately the moral legitimacy of the mission.

A core message of this book, however, is that the Tiwi also turned things upside down. They too played with categories – black and white, pagan and Catholic – to achieve changes for their communities. Flipping norms and expectations were not reserved for white missionaries alone. So this book is also about the way people and communities 'turned' themselves. That is, conversions.

My other academic interest is histories of religion. So I came to the Tiwi Islands with a question: how come, after everything that has happened, some 78 per cent of Tiwi identify as Catholic?[5] Is it fair to say the Tiwi were successfully converted?

Conversion is a slippery concept. The psychologist of religion Lewis Rambo thought of it in terms of 'turning', towards or away from religious communities, beliefs, behaviours or deities.[6] Others describe it as 'crossing' boundaries to search for belonging, not so much about finding 'salvation' or settling on a fixed belief, as if you have somehow 'arrived' at a spiritual destination, but about experimenting and entering new territory. To these writers, conversion is about recreating and reimagining yourself.[7] More than 'travel', conversion also involves 'an encultured being arriving at a particular place'.[8] As people take these journeys, they bring their particular cultures with them and, in turn, encounter the cultures of others. Conversion means cultures get tangled up together.

Thinking about conversion this way is helping scholars understand the history of how Indigenous peoples around the world embraced Christianity while upholding their existing traditions. In the past, 'salvage' anthropologists thought that Indigenous Christianities were just pathetic corruptions of Indigenous cultures, of little cultural worth. Nowadays, most scholars conclude that Indigenous peoples creatively incorporated Christianity into their worlds and that their longstanding traditions live on.[9]

In Australia, First Nations experiences have largely been overlooked in scholarship about Christianity and conversion until recently. Some thinkers have suggested that Christian doctrines and Aboriginal cosmologies are so vastly different that Aboriginal people are unlikely to convert to Christianity.[10] Yet Aboriginal theologians themselves have described their *Dreaming* as compatible with Christian ideas.[11] Many Aboriginal people created ways of being Christian and upholding their distinct spiritual insights about Country.[12] Through history, First Nations people themselves spread Christian teachings to their kin, and some even sought to convert whites. In the 1920s, David Unaipon, for instance, set out to explain his culture to whites, even as he preached Christianity.[13] Djiniyini

Gondarra wrote of sharing the Aboriginal experience of revival with spiritually destitute white people: 'Black preachers and evangelists have preached many years to convert the white church … we want them to be free'.[14] The Tiwi, too, converted their missionaries in their own way. As we shall see, they made them turn and see things differently.

Nowadays, scholars more often explain the history of Christian missions around the world as a more complex back-and-forth whereby Indigenous people creatively incorporated new ideas and practices, often to resist the very imperial powers that sought to dominate them.[15] Of course, this is an improvement on earlier accounts that praised pious missionary adventurers, and much more nuanced than simplistic 'culture clash' versions of mission history. My concern, though, is that this understanding might overshadow Indigenous people's own conceptions of their histories, imposing non-Indigenous categories and theories on Indigenous experiences. Non-Indigenous people like me need to learn to listen to Indigenous societies on their own terms, not through the lens of their colonisers (something I am still learning). Only by doing this can we see Indigenous peoples as having full agency in their own history, rather than simply reacting to whatever Europeans were doing. So how do Tiwi people understand this history of change?

The authors and this book

I am coming to all this as a white woman and a feminist historian. I do have a personal connection to Northern Territory history. My great-grandfather, Quentin Herbert Rice, was a Darwin public servant at the time Gsell was 'buying' his wives. Rice, meanwhile, was caught up in his own dubious transactions concerning Aboriginal people. He was found to be faking Aboriginal signatures, funnelling their earnings to a buffalo-shooting friend. Rice and Gsell knew each other and even had a joint party in 1920 at the Catholic Club.

In the Tiwi way of finding connections, Mavis tells me that my ancestor and hers must have known each other. And they probably did, but I doubt they were friends. Whatever their connection, the truth is my ancestors were part of the Territory's history of exploiting Aboriginal people. I also am not Catholic myself. After two generations of 'mixed' marriages, little of the Catholic tradition made it down to me. But I am a practising Christian, part of the Anglican church. I have long been interested in the history of Christian missions precisely because of the dissonance between my faith and my growing awareness of Christian involvement in Aboriginal dispossession through missions. My church is complicit. So, as much as this book depends on Tiwi voices, I do not and cannot speak for Aboriginal people.

I also have a confession to make at this point. This book began as something else. It too was converted by Tiwi. Although I always intended to use Tiwi oral history, I was led to full co-creation with Tiwi historians. Many of the relevant archival records are closed to researchers. I made extensive use of the archives of the Missionaries of the Sacred Heart in Kensington, Sydney, and the National Archives of Australia, but when it came to the records of the Diocese of Darwin, I learned they were closed as they were being relocated to a cyclone-proof facility. Years later, I learned that there were no documents in the records, only a few unlabelled photographs. The diocesan archives are under-resourced (and this is fair enough; how can a diocese prioritise funds for archives when so many of its Aboriginal parishioners live in poverty?), but I also suspected a wariness, in the wake of inquiries into religious institutions, to share historical records with researchers.

I had similar troubles with the nuns. The Daughters of Our Lady of the Sacred Heart did not want me to view any kind of personal information relating to the sisters. They were always friendly, and I assured them I had no wish to embarrass anyone, but the answer was always 'no'.

The nuns write themselves out of history deliberately. It is part of their vow of humility. They were and are committed to not drawing attention to themselves, going unnoticed. Their constitution called them to be 'unknown':

> [The Sisters] shall deem themselves happy to be weak and poor and unknown or despised, being hidden in God in keeping with the maxim in the Imitation, 'Love to be unknown and esteemed as naught'.[16]

This was unlike the priests, they told me. The Mother Provincial told me that 'if a priest blew his nose we'd know about it, but it wasn't like that for the sisters'. Few sisters consented to be interviewed and I did not see their archives. As a feminist historian, I was frustrated. Still, this is their wish and something I had to accept.

Turning to Tiwi historians

If I wanted to learn anything about the so-called 150 wives, I would not learn it from colonial archives or from speaking to nuns. I would learn it from Tiwi people. So, in 2015, I came to Wurrumiyanga to sit down with the older Tiwi women and ask whether they wanted to share the story. Would they tell it to me and was it okay for me to share it with others? I sat down with Fiona Kerinaiua and Ancilla Kurrupuwu, along with Mavis.

It was not enough, they told me, simply to interview the old women and include Tiwi voices in this history. I needed to work with Tiwi people. Tiwi should be the historians. They were right, of course. So I asked them to work with me. The project was born again.

Mavis came on as co-author, with Fiona and Ancilla as cultural advisers. Since then, we have been working together and learning from each other. I came with my academic approach, they brought their Tiwi cultural knowledge. We are all historians, but we are learning each other's cultures of sharing history; that is, each other's ways of telling and knowing the past, and we hope to make a contribution to both sets of historical knowledge in turn. It was experimental. Our process was for Mavis and me to interview other Tiwi and discuss what we learned together. I would make a start at writing and send the draft to Mavis. She read and re-read, correcting my misunderstandings, querying my prose, instructing me of what is better left unwritten and filling the gaps, such that it was no longer clear where my writing started and hers took over. Fiona and Ancilla read over our work, guiding as we needed. We took the drafts to Tiwi kin too. Is this okay? Should we say this? Have we got it right? Do we have permission? Inevitably, some mistakes remain. Some might wish we'd written things differently. Some might be disappointed we could not include every story and all their kin by name. But, as much as we could, we sought to do things the proper way.

Interviewing Tiwi people about history was a joy. Tiwi people know it, love it and are keen to share it. As I discovered, there is a kind of Tiwi historical canon which, so far, has not been put in writing. These are important stories about the past that answer questions for today. When I asked 'how do Tiwi culture and Catholic faith fit together?' I was not given a theology lecture. I got a history lesson. These stories change slightly with each person and across the generations. This Tiwi historical canon forms the core of this book.

These opening chapters have been written by Mavis and me individually – giving you a chance to get to know us on our own – but after this, we write together, alternating between mini-chapters told directly by Tiwi narrators and chapters Mavis and I prepared together. We begin with Tiwi accounts of how they repelled the British and Dutch from their country. Then we move to stories of how Gsell ingratiated himself with the Tiwi. Following is the story of the first of the 150 'wives': Martina. Next is the Second World War and how the fraught Tiwi relationship with the mission shaped the direction of Australia's experience of war. Then come the mixed memories of the mission days. The mission was both haven and prison, a place of joy and pain. Finally, we close with a story which shows how the Tiwi turned the Catholic mission Tiwi. There were conversions on the Tiwi Islands, but not the ones you might expect.

In oral history, interviewees are inescapably self-selecting; we could only talk with people who wanted to talk with us. Many of the Tiwi historians we include here are Mavis's relatives. They adopted me too, and I became kin in the Tiwi way. White authors can fall into the habit of suggesting that being adopted by Indigenous people gives unique insight into First Nations cultures. It does not. My adoption is not even really about me. It is for Tiwi. It means that Tiwi people know where I fit: they know who I need to respect and who is responsible for keeping an eye on me. It also meant that my Tiwi kin took me under their wings, and their voices will be represented more loudly in this book.

Wurrumiyanga, the old mission, is on Mavis's family's Country – the Country of the Mantiyupwi clan. So this book is really more about Wurrumiyanga and the mission than a story of all Tiwi people. I'm interested in missions and religion, so naturally the mission story is more of a focus. We are sorry we could not include everything and everyone. We touch on the story of the Garden Point Mission, but that story of stolen children deserves a whole book in itself. Think of this book as a taster of Tiwi history. There is much more to tell.

Some might say oral history is limited by the unreliability of memory. But I think sometimes the very 'inaccuracies' of memory are actually useful because they point to the deeper significance of historical events for a community. In historian Alessandro Portelli's words, oral sources 'lead us through and beyond facts to their meanings'.[17] Oral history is also vital as a way of recognising Aboriginal historical knowledge and understanding and to avoid reproducing a power relationship in the past that might silence Aboriginal voices. It also helps academic historians like me to foreground Aboriginal people's concerns and read their priorities into the colonial archive. So in this book, we prioritise oral history over the western archive; Tiwi historians come first.

This approach also means acknowledging lived spiritual realities in Tiwi lives. Secular academia – my world – tends to explain away people's religious experiences as phenomena of underlying social, material or political factors, rather than considering the spiritual world itself as a motivator in people's lives. I follow the example of Robert Orsi, a pioneer in the English-speaking world of the study of 'lived religion'. He discussed the challenge of including spiritual powers as actors in persons' lives and so agents in history.[18] We can keep structural and cultural contexts in mind while also acknowledging that interior, spiritual processes shape religious experience; spirituality is never experienced in a vacuum. The spiritual world profoundly shaped the experiences and motivations of Tiwi people and missionaries alike, even as these experiences occurred in relationships of unequal power and context of colonialism. Since the spiritual mattered to them, we seek to understand it on their terms.

The original woman

According to Tiwi history, Martina was not the first Tiwi woman to leave her husband and change everything for Tiwi people. That was Pima, a Tiwi Creative Being, the curlew bird.

Her story is from long ago, 'parlingari' as Tiwi say, back when all the animals lived on earth like human beings, everyone was happy and nobody died. This is her story:

> A long time ago, a woman named Pima left her baby son,
> Jirnani, at the camp and went gathering food alone. Her
> husband, Purrukuparli, was away hunting. While she was in the
> bush, she met her lover, Japarra, her husband's younger brother.
>
> They stayed together in the bush a long time.

The sun moved higher and higher in the sky. As the shade moved the baby came under the hot sun. Pima wanted to go back to him, but each time she tried, Japarra grabbed her and made her stay with him.

The baby died.

Purrukuparli returned from hunting and found his son dead. When Pima and Japarra finally came back to the camp, he was in a rage.

'Yira waya jumukura nginja-mwarti', 'your son died,' he said. Pima started to cry.

'Ngiya jiringa tinga', 'I'm a bad woman.'

Purrukuparli beat Pima with a stick. He beat her so hard she was transformed into a curlew bird. She still cries out every evening.

Japarra asked Purrukuparli to give him the body of the dead child. 'Give me that baby so I'll bring him back to life on the third day.'

But Purrukuparli would not. 'Ngiya karluwu ngimanginjakirayi kirijini', 'I won't give you my son.' Instead, they fought and fought. They fought until Purrukuparli hit Japarra in the eye and killed him. Japarra went up, into the sky, and became the moon. Every month he dies and returns in three days.

Purrukuparli took his son's body and told everyone, 'you must make ceremony poles and then you will have to dance'. Then he walked out into the sea. 'We will all follow my son. No one will ever come back. Everyone will die.' The water rose up, and the sea took him.[19]

In the story, a woman's desire creates conflict and, ultimately, brings death. As a westerner and a Christian, it is hard not to hear the Tiwi story of love and death – Pima and her baby – without hearing echoes of Christian, Classical and Ancient Near Eastern stories within it. Is this the alluring Aboriginal Eve who causes the fall of humanity, bringing death to all people? Or is she Mary with an innocent baby, an innocent death and a hope of life and resurrection on the third day? Think of Pandora, another 'original' woman, bringing suffering and chaos for her lack of self-control. Or perhaps, as a feminist might read her, she is another victim of patriarchal misrepresentation, the most ancient in a long history of everything supposedly always being a woman's fault.

But to jump to Christian or western meanings here, making Pima into Eve, Pandora, Mary or whoever else, is to miss Pima's side of the story, putting her into a ready-made script about women, especially First Nations women, innocence or victimhood. That is, the kind of story that Gsell invented in his account of Tiwi history, and precisely the kind of story that this book seeks to unpick. So, through this book, I hope that outsiders (including me) can listen to Tiwi women like Pima; that is, to Tiwi historians. And they will have plenty to tell us.

3

JUST LIKE CAPTAIN COOK

Barry Puruntatameri

I strolled down in the village there, where old people were sitting, they were talking about Fort Dundas [Melville Island]. They said this old fella, I heard it from his grand-grand-grand-grandfather. When the first British came they were looking for water. They pull up at Garden Point, at Port Dundas, and they were looking for water, and they dug up a well. The well is still there today. They dug up the well, and they found just a little bit of water, to survive. But actually, the old fella [Tampuwu], they held him as a prisoner, and they threw him in the well.[1]

He was healthy and muscly, you know, his body was built like Hercules, his chest like that there. This is what the story I was told. He was a really young, strong man.

The Dutch was the first to discover Australia, it was on Melville, Captain Cook was later, Johnny-come-lately, yes.

[When the Dutch came] 'this is a strange people in this island', [the Tiwi] said, 'in our Country'. So they found them there, they found them and they chased them all with the spear, they chase them with the spear. They bolted, they went to their own sailing ship and took off, they took off and apparently after that, they never come back.

They didn't come back, they never come back, not like one at Fort Dundas what the Dutch is. This is the British mob arrived on Melville, the British mob, but the Dutch is back 300 years before, they came to Melville, Snake Bay. Three hundred years, and Captain Cook was only 200 years ago.

British was different. They want to fight Aborigine Tiwi mob. They didn't even try how to be friendly to Aborigine, no. The British did, yeah, he was just like Captain Cook. He landed here in Botany Bay and shot all the Indigenous people. That's the history of it. But, this one, when they left, they were going to come back again, the British, when they came to Fort Dundas, and they named that place Fort Dundas.

And that Tampuwu, he was a big man, he escaped from a well. I don't know how he escaped, but he escaped. He climbed up through the well, and he escaped. They tried to chase him and shot him, he already underwater. He escaped and went through the mangroves, they couldn't find, they rode the dinghy looking for him, toward, but they couldn't, he was already left, they told all his Tiwi mob. That's why they chased them with the spear.

They found him by himself down there, they found him by himself, they were looking round for hunting, he was hunting, doing hunting for food, bush tucker, and they found him there, and they grabbed him. They put a chain on him.

His Country was on the other side. He used to go round for hunting, but the Tiwi mob never stop in one place, see, when the food ran out, bush tucker, and the water, and they used to move out where there was plenty of water, bush, plenty of food. And they camped there. Yeah, they sent message stick, they said, 'We're coming', they tell him, send him back, 'Yes, you come', but that was relation, they were all family, there we was all family, relation.

4

TURNING TRESPASSERS

Laura Rademaker
& Mavis Kerinaiua

The Tiwi have been seen as some of the most culturally isolated people in the world. Their minimal contact with outsiders played into western fantasies about Indigenous peoples' survival in a pristine state, supposedly 'untouched' until the late 19th century. 'The most marginal of marginal', as one 20th-century anthropologist put it.[1]

But their isolation was not complete. The Tiwi had plenty of opportunities to meet different cultures over the past few centuries; traders from South East Asia, European explorers, British convicts, buffalo hunters and, naturally, other Aboriginal peoples, all came and went. Plenty of outside peoples had dealings with the Tiwi.

Tiwi do not consider themselves isolated. They were not cut off from the rest of the world, as if the Tiwi Islands were some backwater, far from anywhere. Quite the opposite; the Tiwi Islands are ideally located as a stepping stone from the Australian mainland to South East Asia. But they did defend their sovereignty fiercely, fighting off anyone with designs to exploit them or their land. They told trespassers to go away. This included, most spectacularly, the British Navy. As we shall see, the Tiwi can claim the rare honour of having defeated the navy that 'ruled the waves' in the name of defending their Country.

Tiwi culture is distinct from that of other Aboriginal peoples. Though the Tiwi are made up of various Country groups across the two main islands (Bathurst and Melville Islands, 'Ratuwati Yinjara' – or 'two islands' – in Tiwi), they all speak a common language: Tiwi. Their language is only remotely related to languages on the mainland, just 80 kilometres away. Linguists estimate that their language departed from other Aboriginal languages some 8000 years ago.[2] That would be around the time the sea level rose, after the last ice age, cutting the islands off from the mainland. Today, about 3000 people speak Tiwi, making it one of Australia's strongest, most vibrant Aboriginal languages. Keeping it strong like this remains one of the Tiwi's most important cultural values today. Like other Aboriginal people, Tiwi people have a kinship system that orders their marriage and relationships, but it too is unique. It is matrilineal; that is, you inherit your totem through your mother, not your father, as is common for many other neighbouring Aboriginal peoples. But your Country, or land affiliation, comes from your father.

The Tiwi have known their mainland neighbours – the Iwaidja (from the Cobourg Peninsula) and the Larrakia (from the Darwin region) people – since forever. Their Countries were only a canoe-paddle away (albeit through strong, dangerous currents that later wrecked many European vessels) and clearly visible from their islands. The Old People (the Ancestors) knew how to speak Iwaidja.[3] Sometimes relations were friendly, other times not. Men and women often had different perspectives on the matter: it's complicated. Tiwi women had long taken an interest in mainland men, and Tiwi men in the women. There were many wars. The most recent was in the 1860s when both sides tried to 'steal' women (or did the women elope?).[4] Tiwi historian Romolo Kantilla explained to us what his elders told him about those days:

The young men would have travelled across in a canoe to the mainland and declared war on the local Darwin tribe, the Larrakia tribe. To do that, we steal their wives and bring them back here.[5]

The Macassans and the trepang trade

Tiwi relations with others in the region goes back centuries. The Macassans (from modern-day Indonesia) journeyed to North Australia on the annual north-westerly dry-season winds. They came to harvest trepang (sea slugs or *bêche-de-mer*), trading with Aboriginal people of North Australia. The trepang industry was owned by the Chinese and operated to satisfy the huge Chinese demand for what they considered a delicacy (Macassans and Aboriginal people disagreed; they would not eat the stuff). So Chinese business interests in Australia pre-date those of Europeans.

The Macassans came for hundreds of years. Archaeologist Anne Clarke dates Macassan campsites in North Australia at around 800 years old.[6] They came in fleets of up to 60 vessels with crews of 30, remaining for the wet season and returning on the south-easterly dry-season winds. Macassan crews were multicultural and multilingual. Most were Macassarese speakers from Macassar in Sulawesi, but crew members also came from Borneo, Timor, Java, New Guinea and other parts of North Australia. The crews spoke Malay Creole, a language based upon Sumatran and Malay languages with a strong Portuguese influence. Some Aboriginal people travelled widely with the Macassans on their journeys and stayed in Macassar for years at a time.[7]

Although the Macassans established long-lasting relationships (sometimes positive, sometimes less so) with other Aboriginal peoples, this seems not to have happened on the Tiwi Islands. The Macassans certainly visited. The tamarind trees from Malaysia on the islands are a prominent physical reminder of their visits. Tiwi historical memory also features the Macassans. It was Macassans who first brought tobacco, so there was, at some time, a Tiwi–Macassan trade.[8] Tiwi people remember that Macassans 'didn't come with the guns' like Europeans but with 'rice, axes, knives'.[9] Today, the Tiwi language contains Macassan words and Old People today remember their grandparents could speak Macassan. As Tiwi historian and artist Bede Tungutalum explained:

> And so all the Macassans came. There are some, some of my people speak, they all gone now. One was my uncle. He lived at Garden Point. He died two years ago. He's the only one speak Macassan ... I speak a little bit. I can understand like a little, you know but, I can't speak properly. We all learn speak Macassan. We used some of that language. Combination ... They came here, they brought Tamarind trees as well ... There's a lot of swear word, I don't want to say it ... I know the swear words, as well. And they used to say it. And we learn from these people, we picked up, we learnt this. I used to pick up what he was saying, but he's fluently speak. Macassans they [Tiwi] invite them in ... Only fought the British and the Dutch.[10]

By the 1820s, the Macassans no longer came to the Tiwi Islands on their annual voyages to Australia, visiting other Aboriginal communities instead. Perhaps this is because the dangerous currents and reefs surrounding the Tiwi Islands were not worth the risk.

The Portuguese

According to rumour, the first white people to come to the islands were the Portuguese. Some say the Portuguese – or perhaps their Timorese agents – captured Tiwi to sell as slaves across the Indian Archipelago. The evidence for such a slave trade is patchy.[11] It is based on the conjecture of 19th-century Englishmen about their former imperial rivals; they were unlikely to portray the Portuguese in a flattering light. In 1818, naval officer Phillip Parker King heard Tiwi women beckoning 'ven aca, ven aca' and interpreted this as the Portuguese 'venha aqui'; that is, 'come here'.[12] Perhaps they had met the Portuguese and could speak a little of their language. Major

John Campbell encountered a Tiwi man who mimed as if struggling to escape with hands enchained and motioned as if being hung by the neck. Campbell took this as evidence that the Tiwi had been enslaved (not, curiously, as evidence that the Tiwi had observed Campbell's own treatment of convicts). Campbell also noted that Macassan sailors called Melville Island 'Amba', which he believed meant 'slave' in their language. He noticed a boy who looked Asian, perhaps Malay, living with the Tiwi. This was also evidence, to him, that Tiwi might have taken the boy from 'some Malay slave ship'.[13] But Tiwi have long had relations with various peoples from across South East Asia through their Macassan visitors. Plenty of Tiwi have Asian ancestry. Another explanation for the boy's appearance could be that a Tiwi mother found the Malays attractive, but Campbell did not consider the possibility of friendly relations, only slavery.

Beyond this, there is not much evidence for a trade of enslaved Tiwi people. Few Tiwi talk about the Portuguese; if they had been enslaved, it's likely there would be more stories about it. Perhaps the British colonisers, on their attempt to seize Tiwi land without permission or compensation, found comfort in imagining that some even more terrible fate had befallen the Tiwi in the past. This would make the British conquest seem relatively benign. If the rumours are true and the Portuguese did in fact enslave the Tiwi, then the Tiwi's first encounter with the Catholic faith would have been as slaves.

The anti-Dutch alliance

There is more certainty about Tiwi encounters with the Dutch. As Tiwi historian Barry Puruntatameri explained in the previous chapter:

> Dutch was the first to discover Australia, it was on Melville, Captain Cook was later, Johnny-come-lately.[14]

In 1636, the Dutch merchant Pieter Pieterszoon sailed near Melville Island. He sighted land and fire, but no people. When he paddled along the shores of the islands, even landing at points, he saw no one. But the Tiwi saw him. Abel Tasman followed, sailing along the north coast of the islands in 1644. He saw the islands from a distance, but did not land.[15] Then, in 1705, the Dutch East India Company sent Maarten van Delft from Batavia to the region.

When van Delft and his crew first landed on the Tiwi Islands, everyone – women, men, children and dogs – ran away. Then they strategised. Soon after, a party of 15 armed Tiwi men ran at them, signalling 'go away!' The sailors did not. So the Tiwi men threw their spears. The sailors retaliated. One fired a musket and hit a Tiwi man. 'They shot that one Tiwi man. They shot him in the leg', the Tiwi remember. The warriors dispersed, for the time being. The sailors assisted and bandaged the wounded man, but he refused to accept this gesture, tearing the linen to pieces. So the sailors tried to pacify the Tiwi, inviting some aboard the ship, offering food and gifts – beads, knives and linen – but the Tiwi kept fighting the trespassers, wounding two. The Dutch concluded the Tiwi had nothing of value to them (they had hoped to find precious metals or spices) and noted that Tiwi people had no desire to see them again, commenting 'the nature of these tribes is foul and treacherous'.[16]

Barry Puruntatameri remembered Tiwi impressions of the Dutch. They noticed that their skin was 'different', 'as white as a paperbark tree, that colour'.[17] Different Tiwi groups who were normally rivals, 'they all joined together', forging a new alliance.

The reason Tiwi fought together was simple. In the words of Tiwi elder Bede Tungutalum, they were 'not allowed, foreigners [were] not allowed'.[18] Today the Tiwi memorialise the Dutch encounter in their dance tradition, making the sign of a ship's mast. As Richard Tungutalum told it:

My great, great grandfather still hold, because he can [do] the song and the dance in front of the ship. And they do the farewell dance, who do the mast.[19]

The 'Johnny-come-lately' British

Then the British arrived. The Tiwi memorialise this encounter in song and dance too. It took the British longer to realise just how unwelcome they were. Their attempted colony on the Tiwi Islands lasted five years: from 1824 to 1829. Puruntatameri explained, 'the British came with the bang! Bang! Bang! Bang!'[20] In the words of another Tiwi historian, Richard Tungutalum, 'they didn't stay long'.[21]

The grand plan was to build 'another Singapore'.[22] Just as present-day Australian governments still dream of 'developing the North' to crack into Asian markets, the English in the 1820s saw the Tiwi Islands as strategically located to introduce European commodities into trade networks across the Indian Archipelago and up to China.[23] Matthew Flinders charted the north coast of Australia and encountered the Tiwi Islands in 1803. Following him, Lieutenant Phillip Parker King surveyed the islands in 1818.

King's party landed on Melville Island. But as they sized up the islands, the party was so startled by a group of Tiwi warriors that they abandoned their surveying equipment and ran for their boat. Cautiously, that afternoon, King and the Tiwi traded tomahawks for fruit. But when the Englishmen signalled that they wanted their surveying equipment returned, the Tiwi found another opportunity. Perhaps the Tiwi had a sense of why the English so desired these objects, suspecting the English plan to acquire their islands. A Tiwi woman went out in the water, waist-deep, carrying the equipment. King claimed not to think much of her looks. Nonetheless, when she signalled, 'come here', the sailors followed her towards land, and as they did so, two Tiwi men reached to take a tomahawk. Later, another Tiwi woman beckoned and, as the sailors once again approached, Tiwi men nearby reached for their submerged spears. King's crew was spooked by the women and the warriors and they left the Tiwi alone.[24]

King's survey piqued imperial commercial interests. There would be a British naval settlement on the island 'to establish a commercial intercourse with the natives of various islands in the Indian Archipelago' via the Macassan trepangers, who, they incorrectly presumed, still visited the islands for the annual harvest.[25] The British wanted to take North Australia before their colonial rivals (the French and Dutch) did. Moreover, establishing a base there would allow them to circumvent the trade monopolies of the Dutch and East India Companies in the region.[26] A British naval and commercial base would connect Sydney to southern China, Indonesia and Singapore. The Colonial Office, therefore, dispatched instructions to the Admiralty and, in 1824, Captain Gordon Bremer was appointed to the task.[27]

His ship was called the *Tamar*. It landed at Garden Point (now Pirlangimpi) in September 1824 and established the settlement of 'Fort Dundas'. Bremer's fleet included around 100 people: 45 of them convicts, 26 Royal Marines, 24 foot troops, one surgeon, a handful of mechanics and officers and the others farmers. The convicts were a diverse group. At least one of them was Aboriginal. At least two were women. Thirteen were of African descent.[28] Their arrival is memorialised in Tiwi tradition: there is a Tiwi dance which re-enacts the arrival of ships and men rowing ashore.[29]

At this stage, the British Empire had not yet asserted sovereignty over the Tiwi Islands. The colony of New South Wales extended westwards only as far as 135 degrees east (that is, down the middle of the Northern Territory of today). The Tiwi themselves were the islands' only claimants.

The audacity of the British is stunning. Landing on the beach, planting a flag and firing a cannon, James Gordon Bremer claimed not only the Tiwi Islands, but the whole northern coast of Australia, for George IV in 1824:

The North Coast of New Holland of Australia ... were taken
possession of, in the name and in the right of His Most Excellent
Majesty George IV ... at Melville and Bathurst Islands on
the 26th September, 1824, by James John Gordon Bremer,
Companion of the most honourable Military Order of the Bath,
Captain of His Majesty's Ship the Tamar, and Commanding
Officer of His Majesty's Forces, employed on the said Coasts.[30]

The Tiwi, of course, never accepted this. But the colonists got busy
inscribing Tiwi places with names which spoke of British military
might. They named Melville Island for Viscount Melville, Head of
the Admiralty. Bathurst Island was for Earl Bathurst, Secretary of
State for the Colonies.[31] Viscount Melville double dipped; Dundas
was also one of his names, so Fort Dundas was his too. Missionary
John Pye noted that there is also a Melville Island, a Bathurst Island
and a Dundas in North Canada; the names spoke of a global empire
and subjected peoples across the earth under the one imperial rule.[32]
Though the fort on the Tiwi Islands did not last long, the settlement
and claim there was a stepping stone for the British to keep moving
westwards, eventually claiming the whole Australian continent for
their empire.[33]

One of the first things the British noticed was the Tiwi Pukumani poles, the ceremonial grave posts intricately carved with motifs
that trace the deceased's spiritual identity. They stand watch over the
graves of the dead. The British were impressed. By their reckoning,
judging by the poles, Tiwi culture must be more sophisticated than
other Aboriginal peoples' because the Tiwi, like Europeans, bury
their dead. For Bremer, the poles meant that the Tiwi must not be
'as rude and barbarous' as other Aboriginal people. He decided that
they must believe in God, or at least some 'Superior Power'; why
else would they create such elaborate memorials for the dead?[34] The
European assumption that Tiwi people were just a little closer to
God than other Aboriginal people made them an ideal people for a
Catholic mission, nearly a century later.

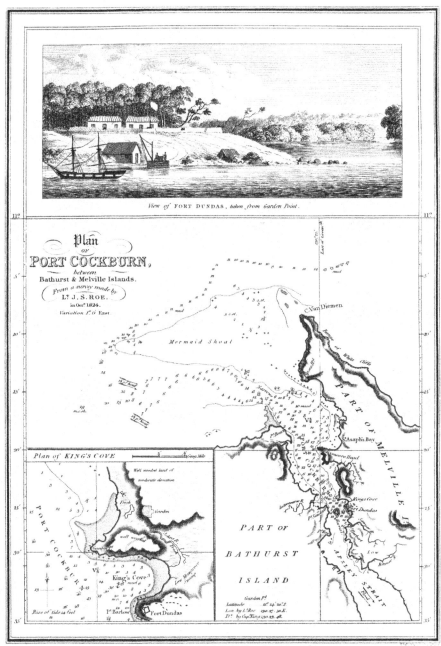

View of Fort Dundas from Garden Point, 1825.
John Murray, Northern Territory Library

The first thing Bremer did was build a fort (or, more precisely, arrange for the convicts to build a fort). He expected 'treacherous' Malays and 'hostile' natives, so was 'determined to make the Fort as strong as my means would permit'.[35] As Richard Tungutalum explained, 'British didn't respect tribal boundaries'. They didn't do 'the right thing' and broke Tiwi law around trespassing.[36] Tiwi historian James Darren Puantulura explained that the Tiwi were happy to trade with the British at first, but when they did not respect Tiwi women, that was the end of the friendship:

> They was trading for food, and smokes and everything, flour,
> and plus woman, and that's why that conflict came with woman,
> because they want to take woman back to Britain … That's why
> they were happy for people to burn that place, destroy that camp,
> and the British camp, destroy them all.[37]

The British also cut the native grass. This destroyed the feed for wallabies, which they also hunted in competition with Tiwi hunters. They cleared 52 acres of timber, a considerable part of the land's resources. Their livestock was not suited to the Tiwi climate but they cleared the land for 'their camel and other animals they brought from the freezing country'.[38] As the dry season approached, the British control over the fresh water supply was also alarming for Tiwi. Unlike the Dutch or the Macassans, these trespassers had come in much larger numbers: it looked as if they intended to stay permanently. The Tiwi had 'had enough'.[39] It was time to 'fight them to get rid of them'.[40]

The Tiwi guerrilla strategy

On Bremer's first encounter with Tiwi, an armed party of Tiwi men approached with spears. He offered them 'a handkerchief and some other trifles'. The Tiwi warriors left 'apparently well satisfied'.

The peace was short-lived. That afternoon, a party of Tiwi people surrounded two of the colonists, wrestling their axes from them but leaving them otherwise unharmed. The colonists fled to the fort, the soldiers raised their muskets, the Tiwi bolted. The soldiers intended harm: 'some of the Natives would have Suffered [*sic*] for their temerity if they had not hastily retreated', Bremer recounted.[41]

Tiwi people requested axes, perhaps as compensation, perhaps insisting on reciprocity, miming the action of cutting down trees. Bremer told them 'they should have axes, if they came to the Settlement'. They came near, but would not enter. Some Tiwi had likely been kidnapped and imprisoned by this stage, so they knew they were not safe. They received no axes. So, after the colonisers refused their request, the Tiwi took (the colonists said 'stole') three.[42] Another time, the Tiwi seized an axe and reaping hook. According to Bremer, when he saw 'the Savages preparing to throw their spears; the Corporal thought it right to fire over their heads'. The Tiwi fighters withdrew. But the corporal continued, loading as he ran, 'firing repeatedly'. The Tiwi retaliated with a 'Shower of Spears', injuring the midshipman. So, the corporal aimed to kill. Bremer's description is telling:

> It was now necessary to convince them that they were inferior, and for the Sake of sparing bloodshed, which would have followed another discharge of Spears, the Corporal selected the Chief for punishment and fired directly at him; he immediately fell or threw himself to the ground (which several others constantly did on Seeing the flash of the piece); but it was most probably that he was struck by the ball, for he did not rise so quickly as the rest; the whole party ran into the thick wood, and, as since that period none have been seen in the neighbourhood of the Settlement or watering place.[43]

Seizing the colonisers' tools was part of the Tiwi guerrilla strategy. Other tactics were setting haystacks alight, spearing livestock, destroying fences, seizing washing left out on the line. They threw spears into the huts and the hospital; nowhere was safe.[44] The colonisers were under siege. Their leaders instructed them not to leave the fort alone or unarmed. They lived with the constant threat of a Tiwi ambush. The Tiwi kept the colonisers constantly on edge; one day they were friendly, allowing colonists to pass by safely, the next, they would attack without warning. They set traps. Sometimes they approached the settlement, apparently unarmed, and convinced the colonists to lay down their weapons and come towards them in peace, then they took up their spears and waddies (a waddy is a club or hunting stick) hidden behind trees for a surprise attack.[45]

The Tiwi were practised at sneak attacks. Killing in a sneak attack (jurraga, 'to sneak up and kill') – perhaps at night or just before dawn – was a Tiwi tactic, still common until the mission times.[46] Secrecy and deception were well-honed techniques. 'Tricking them, tricking them', as James Darren Puantulura explained.[47] The Tiwi were used to taking measures to protect themselves from attacks like this. They knew, for instance, to sleep hiding among the mangroves. The British did not:

> They didn't know the Country, they had to go in and come out with a tricky place, with an easy place, with the hardest place. That's why those Tiwi mob that was really clever ... This Tiwi mob had a clever way of doing. We outsmart those guns. We outsmart them.[48]

Major Campbell remembered attempts to communicate. 'Co curdy' meant 'water' or 'I am thirsty'. The Tiwi word for fresh water is 'kukuni': he was not too far off. They said 'piccanini' for 'children'. 'Piccanini' is not a Tiwi word, but it is common to pidgin languages across the region. Where had they learned it? Perhaps Campbell had inadvertently introduced it. Or had they learned it from the Macassans? Or other Aboriginal people? Given they knew how to communicate, if only a little, with these intruders, the Tiwi could not have been as isolated as has been thought.

Tiwi women, meanwhile, avoided the British altogether. Campbell claimed the British only saw two Tiwi women in the whole four years on the island. Both were reportedly 'old and ugly'.[49] Perhaps, for Campbell, the absence of island women indicated the place's supposed barrenness and inhospitality for the British. But why did women stay away? Tiwi women had been central in brokering relationships with the Macassans and Iwaidja, but with the British, they remained elusive. Perhaps they thought there was no point in acting as cultural brokers with the British. Perhaps they knew the British were dangerous. As James Darren Puantulura told it, the British were known to treat Aboriginal women badly.[50]

Hoping to learn more of the language, the British kidnapped a Tiwi man, Tampuwu Tipungwuti, as their captive.[51] Tampuwu was alone, hunting, when they seized him and enchained him.[52] But this was a mistake.

Tampuwu was a 'big man', a leader. He escaped. Finding a canoe, he paddled to Malawu on the north side of Bathurst Island. According to some Tiwi accounts, he was so strong, he broke his chains. According to others, he refused food until he was so skinny, he slipped through the cuffs.[53] Some learned stories from the Old People about Tampuwu being thrown in a well and escaping.[54] Perhaps he climbed out. Whatever his method, the British blundered by capturing him. Previously the Tiwi were divided by their various clans. But the insult to Tampuwu was enough to unite all Tiwi against the British:

And their chief of that place, get angry and maybe even tell everybody, come here ... oh yeah, we'll go there and kill them all. All tribes around Dundas went there. Fort Dundas. Get a big mob, more soldiers. But when you've got tribes from all around, you game over.[55]

Then, the besieged colonists began to fall sick. Perhaps they were 'cursed' or 'poisoned'. Over a period of two months, six died from illness. Dysentery, blindness and scurvy (they were malnourished). Their gardens had failed to produce a crop. In 1828, Major Campbell sent eight convicts back to Sydney, convinced that they would not survive the coming wet season.[56] The famous 'build up' and wet season of North Australia was too much. As any Territorian will tell you, the humidity drives people mad; today they call it 'mango madness,' and it seems Campbell had a bout of it. 'The closeness of the atmosphere and the extreme unvaried heat has been very oppressive indeed and occasioned uncommon debility', Campbell complained. Then the convicts refused to work. They wanted to leave.[57] They got drunk to the point of rioting. They feigned illness. They swore at their superiors. They refused to give evidence incriminating each other. Perhaps some were beginning to side with the Tiwi. Though some were flogged and imprisoned, their behaviour did not change.[58]

Meanwhile, the Tiwi warriors became bolder. Having seized an axe and saw overnight, they paraded their plunder before the colonisers in the morning and attacked a work party of colonisers with spears and waddies. Then, when the two soldiers guarding the workers opened fire, they did not withdraw as they had formerly done, and only escaped into the forest when a whole party of soldiers from the barracks came out. That night, they attacked an armed sentry with rocks and seized a hand cart.[59]

The Tiwi killed four colonists in total. According to Major Campbell, 'they put two gentlemen of the settlement, one soldier and one of the prisoners [that is, convicts] to death, and wantonly wounded several others'.[60] The escaped Tampuwu informed his compatriots where to attack. Emboldened by his mistreatment, the Tiwi speared the surgeon – the colonists' only doctor – to death, as well as an officer who was walking only a few yards from the settlement.[61]

We do not know exactly how many Tiwi people the invaders killed. Major Campbell reported that 'they had at length been fired upon whilst committing acts of outrage'. He maintained that 'they had been the first aggressors, by throwing spears', neglecting to mention

Iwaidja fighters aiming spears at
Tiwi warrior Edward Reichenbach, 191[?].
Northern Territory Library

the original act of aggression: claiming the Tiwi Islands for the Crown. 'We were obliged to fire at them several times; we never knew of any having been killed, although in one or two instances they were wounded; they might have died'. Though still not admitting to killing any Tiwi people, Campbell conceded that 'the spirit of revenge might have excited [the Tiwi] to other acts of violence', implicitly conceding that the Tiwi forces experienced grave casualties.[62] Explorer Thomas Braidwood Wilson's 1835 memoir looked back on the settlement and commented that 'many of the natives were put to death in a very unwarrantable manner' and blames the colonisers' heavy-handedness for much of the Tiwi resistance. In his view, the 'petty thefts' of the Tiwi did not warrant 'putting them to death'.[63]

Historians debate why the settlement failed. Was it the climate and geography, the absence of trepangers, the sickness or the Tiwi resistance?[64] Most likely, it was the cumulative effect of all of these. Sickness and the subsequent resistance of the convict workforce was part of it. The failure of the long-awaited trepangers to arrive was significant. The British made a serious misjudgement when they thought contact with trepangers on the Tiwi Islands would open Asian markets to them. The soil was not suited to cultivating European crops. The currents of the surrounding seas were dangerous.[65]

But we credit the Tiwi. The Tiwi guerrilla strategy wore the colonisers down, materially and psychologically. The Tiwi exploited their superior knowledge of the island's geography and climate. Armed with spears and waddies, Tiwi fighters faced muskets; their bravery unnerved the colonisers. The surgeon's death in 1828 seems to have been the final straw for the beleaguered colonisers, who abandoned the settlement in 1829. The Tiwi sent the British Navy away, defeated and demoralised.

The Tiwi's power to turn the intruders away becomes even more obvious when you think about how things could have been different. Imagine if the Tiwi had assisted the colonisers instead of attacking: they might have showed them how to find a nutritious diet; they might have provided surveillance and intelligence on the convicts; they might have established positive relations with the Macassans – as other Aboriginal peoples did – and acted as mediators between the Macassans and the British. Fort Dundas, under these circumstances, might have thrived. But the Tiwi people did not do these things. Instead, they fought, and the colonisers left, defeated. In the words of Bede Tungutalum, '[The Old People] fought the English when they came to my land. They fight them to get rid of them. But the British didn't stay long there. They gave up'.[66]

Although the Tiwi were able to keep the British at bay, in other parts of the continent, the colonisers spread and, ever since Bremer fired his cannon, the British considered the Tiwi Islands and the surrounding Country property of the Crown. The colony of South

Australia gained administration of the Northern Territory in 1863. The port of Palmerston – now Darwin – was founded in 1869, only around 50 kilometres from Melville Island. The Tiwi benefited from the many subsequent shipwrecks through the area, gaining iron and cutting tools without cost. But they were vulnerable to further invasions from white people with British backing.

Pearlers and buffalo hunters

Some time in the late 19th century, the Tiwi became acquainted with the crews of pearling luggers which worked in these waters and used their island to re-supply.[67] Some of the boats were owned by Australians, others by Japanese, but the luggers themselves were crewed by Indonesians, Malaysians and Japanese labourers – often indentured. The pearlers gave the Tiwi clothes, tobacco and sugar in return for being allowed to harbour in their waters. The Tiwi, especially some Tiwi women, got on well with these crews.

Then a new type of white man arrived on Melville Island in the 1890s: the buffalo shooter. Back in the 1820s, the British at Fort Dundas had introduced Timorese buffalo to Melville Island. Now a new wave of white men came to hunt them. Joe (Robert) Cooper and Barney Flynn arrived in 1895 with a team of Iwaidja men.[68] At first they were welcome, as Tiwi historian and community leader Bernard Tipiloura explained:

On the other side [that is, on Melville Island] were buffalo. But anyway, this Joe Cooper lived there and he started the buffalo, and that's how the buffalo gone wild on the other side. Yeah, that's the only other – he's not a government, he's not a mission; he's just a buffalo hunter and he live at Paru on the other side [of the Apsley Strait]. They [Tiwi people] welcome [him]. Because of one of my eldest were looking at it, there's food, they had buffalo. Yeah, so they look on, you know, what give people benefit. He know he was white skinned but they all go, 'Oh, he's got something nice in buffalo'.[69]

But the relationship did not last. 'Barney Flynn bin kill lotta people. [He] go along bush, [people] run away'. Tiwi people have various stories about the buffalo hunters. Though the stories vary, they always came to a grisly end. As Romolo Kantilla explains:

> Joe Cooper didn't listen until one day he found his brother with 18 spears in his body. That's when he jumped in the boat and run away.[70]

In 1895, Porkiliari, a Tiwi man, speared Cooper in the shoulder. So the buffalo hunters fled to the mainland, taking with them a group of 12 Tiwi women, men and children.[71] Flynn died on the mainland, apparently from a venomous snakebite. But there was also another poison on him. According to Tiwi stories, he had been 'sung' – with magic poison – by people on the mainland.[72]

Cooper persisted. He, again, set up camp on Melville Island in 1905. He brought a group of Iwaidja men from the mainland to work for him, not only in hunting buffalo but also as bodyguards against Tiwi sneak attacks. He brought Iwaidja women too: 'he's the one who breed a lot of kids [with Iwaidja women], Joe Cooper'. Cooper also came with a Tiwi man, Samuel Ingeruintamiri, to be a mediator. He and his workers had guns. When the workers took an interest in the Tiwi women, the Tiwi men found their spears were no match for the guns. In 1912, the new Chief Protector for Aborigines of the Northern Territory began exiling mainland Aboriginal offenders to Cooper's camp on Melville Island 'to wean them from their drunken habits'.[73] The Tiwi encountered a great influx of unknown Aboriginal people.[74]

Tiwi people remember that Joe Cooper used to place the bodies of people who died (or were they killed?) up on burial platforms. This is a practice from the mainland, but it is not the Tiwi way. Tiwi bury their dead. Cooper's actions were disturbing and inappropriate.[75]

Meanwhile, in 1909, Sam Green, a sawmiller, also based himself on Melville Island. Green started reporting the behaviour of Cooper and his men to the white authorities. A Tiwi man, Billy Muck, had been shot dead. A Tiwi woman had been hung from a tree by her feet for half a day. Another, Harriet, had both her legs broken by a mainlander and later died of her injuries. Dumedibella took a blow to the head from a waddy by a man working for Cooper. Cooper, too, was implicated in the violence. He had kidnapped a Larrakia woman, Mary, wrapping a saddle-strap around her neck, to force her into submission.[76]

> [Joe Cooper] was a really conman. It's a bad thing about, against Tiwi girls, it was a bad, he was a really bad man, but he used to give them food and everything, he said, 'You give me, I'll take your wife', and it was bad, I didn't, when I heard that, I felt inside really bad.[77]

As much as Joe Cooper is known for his atrocities, Tiwi people also keep in mind that he had a big Aboriginal family. His descendants are Tiwi kin. Therefore Tiwi are not antagonistic or vengeful. Instead, they look to their relatedness with their Cooper family as a source of healing from a troubled past.

But ultimately, 'they got rid of him and they said, "No more come back"'.[78] Just as they had done to the Dutch and British before, the Tiwi turned the buffalo hunters away from their Country. They had a lot of problems with trespassers on their land. But this time was different. This time, as we shall see, instead of spears, they used a powerful white man; they adopted a new strategy and turned to the missionary priest.

5

COME AND MEET
THIS FELLA

Romolo Kantilla

I'm going to tell you a background history of Tiwi people. Tiwi people have lived on Bathurst and Melville forever and no one knows how long. We've lived in isolation for so long that our language and culture are totally different from mainland Aboriginals at Katherine and Alice Springs. Tiwi means 'we are one', you know why? 'Cause my people they thought they were the only people on the planet. They call themselves Tiwi, 'one'. They were so isolated from everyone.

The only contact with the outside world was when the young men would have travelled across in a canoe to the mainland and declared war on the local Darwin tribe, the Larrakia tribe. To do that, we steal their wives and bring them back here. That time there was a shortage of women on the island. Women used to swim across back and forth. Only men on the canoe. Women were good swimmers, long time. They used to swim across [to the mainland] to get a mango. The Iwaidja used to come here too.[1] There's no didjeridu, no boomerang on the island. No woomera. But the Iwaidja people they used to come and introduce the didj: ceremony. They used to dance for us too. I just found that out last year, I saw it in a book, I read it. I didn't know that. Iwaidja people used to come.

In 1600 that's when the Macassans came up here north of Australia, north of the island. They landed on Melville Island. That

44

was 1600 the Macassan came. They introduced us to many things: steel axes, dugout canoe, smoking, even playing cards.

In 1705, that's when the Dutch landed on the north coast of Melville Island. My people didn't allow trespassers. So they attacked them, drove them away. And one of the Tiwi men got shot, he got injured. And the Dutchman came back and patched up his wound. He stayed for a while, we made friends. And they left, never returned.

In 1824 that's when the British began settlement, on the north coast of Melville Island at Garden Point. And my people didn't allow trespassers, so they made war on the fort for four and a half years until they left. And they were responsible for a new word in our language for white people, we say murrintawi, which means 'hot red face'.

In 1911, that's when the mission came. The mission played a big role of life on Bathurst Island, taught us many things including Aussie Rules Football. Everyone says AFL is our second religion, but I believe it's our number one religion.

Father Gsell went around both islands and he came back here, saw the big smoke. Saw the Old People. And he gave them food, flour, tobacco. And he told him about the Bible and all that. That's when they sent a message.

The Old People passed the message to the Tiwi people, 'Come and meet this fella, this white man gave me this thing. Come, come and meet mission'. That's when they all came. Some of them left their kids here and went back to the bush. My grandfather left my dad and Marie Carmel's husband, my uncle, left them here at the school and went back bush. Some of them were living bush when the mission came. They didn't come and blend in with their culture. It took ten years for the priest to understand about our culture.

The first settlement before the mission was Joe Cooper. That was the first settlement before the mission, that little village called Paru. He was a buffalo hunter and with him he had a group of Aboriginal people from Arnhem Land, Croker Island. They were buffalo hunters. They used to live there. He and his men got a bit lonely and wanted to steal Tiwi men's wives. And one of the Tiwi men got shot because Cooper and his men had guns and Tiwi men had spears. So one of the Tiwi men got shot. The mission arrived and Father Gsell heard what happened. And he went across, got in his dinghy and told Joe Cooper that 'you gotta control your men, otherwise I'm going to go to the mainland and I'm gonna tell the government what you doing'. Joe Cooper didn't listen until one day he found his brother with 18 spears in his body. That's when he jumped in the boat and run away. Father tried to warn him.

Today we run these islands through the Tiwi Land Council, and they represent all Tiwi people. Any business that wants to come in goes through the Tiwi Land Council, so there's no more trespassers.

6

COME AND SEE

Laura Rademaker
& Mavis Kerinaiua

After a long history – centuries – of removing trespassers from their land, you might wonder why, when the missionaries arrived, the Tiwi did not immediately oppose them. Why did they not turn Gsell back, as they had done with all the others?

The Tiwi themselves sometimes wonder about this. What were their Old People thinking? As Tiwi historian Romolo Kantilla mused, 'I always think about that. Because when I tell the history, how come they didn't, when the mission came, how come they didn't, like, chase them away?'[1]

The Tiwi do have an answer, but, once again, it is not what you might expect. The missionaries brought useful material goods: axes, blankets, flour. There was the strategic element; missionaries had access to powerful white allies. But Tiwi also perceived them as different to other intruders, spiritually and culturally. The Tiwi saw potential in them, and they were curious.

The absence of Catholic missions in Australia

Tiwi historians know the story of Gsell's arrival. The beach was deserted. There was some confusion about his identity. They did not

47

think he was the police. No, 'they thought it was a ghost because he had that long beard, they thought it was a ghost!' The Tiwi also called Gsell Tutiyanginari, that is, 'white clay man'. They said, 'white fella there! Skin like clay!'[2] Teddy Portaminni tells the story:

> He came with his Filipino crewmen. Came over here and he landed there. But then he saw nobody, only saw one man, I think … They all come down. Just to see him. That skin is different. They were curious. Probably a little bit afraid because they saw him and they said, maybe he's a evil spirit.[3]

Tiwi were right to be surprised and concerned by the arrival of this strange character. When Gsell turned up on the Tiwi beach in 1911, it was against the odds. There were not many missionaries to Aboriginal people at the time. Until the 20th century, most missions to Aboriginal people had lasted only a few years, with few (or even no) Aboriginal converts. There were some exceptions, famously the Hermannsburg Mission in Central Australia. But other missions were often isolated attempts by zealous individuals. They struggled to attract finances and converts. European settlers often resented them as competitors for farmland. And normally, the settlers won and missions closed.

Meanwhile, the Aboriginal population across the Australian continent was in catastrophic decline. Violence, disease and forced exile from their land were devastating for many Aboriginal people. In this context, the missions quickly failed, and Aboriginal people had little reason to be interested in Christianity and especially to trust white people.

Catholics in Australia did even less to aid Aboriginal people in the 19th century than their Protestant counterparts.[4] Four Italian Passionist priests established a mission on Stradbroke Island in 1843, but they left after only four years. The New Norcia Spanish Benedictine mission and monastery in Western Australia had far better fortunes, continuing from 1846 to 1974 as an orphanage. There were also three short-lived missions in the north; the first was Italian Don Angelo Confalonieri's mission to the Iwaidja people from 1846 to 1848. He died of malaria and the mission ended. Duncan McNab (a Scotsman) made efforts in Queensland and the Kimberley in the 1870s and 1880s. There was also an Austrian Jesuit mission on the Daly River that survived from 1886 until 1899, when the river flooded and the mission collapsed.

For Aboriginal people in colonial Australia, life on a mission was sometimes the least bad option. That says more about the constant danger they were in and their limited options than the benefits of missions. The missions did present opportunities to gain access to western knowledge, useful skills (such as writing in English), and spirituality, and could be a refuge from violent settlers. Yet the missions also operated with strict discipline and work regimes. Missionaries' views of Aboriginal culture were patronising and racist. Most focused on children, believing adults could not be changed. This could be devastating for Aboriginal families, especially when missionaries forcibly removed children from their kin.

Gsell's arrival on the Tiwi Islands was part of a renewed push to evangelise and provide humanitarian assistance to Aboriginal people in the early 20th century. Churches recognised the living conditions of Aboriginal people as a humanitarian crisis. They looked to Aboriginal people in the far north of Australia who, as yet, had little contact with Europeans. North Australia presented an opportunity to operate with as little interference from other settlers (considered to be a bad influence) as possible. By the 1920s, there were over 20 mission stations in remote parts of North Australia – often isolated islands – with the vision of transforming Aboriginal people into 'civilised' Christians. The idea was to strengthen Aboriginal people with Christianity so that they would survive the coming of Europeans (presumed to be inevitable). Although missionaries hoped to protect Aboriginal people from complete annihilation, they worried they might not succeed. At least, though, they could provide charity and, they believed, 'smooth the dying pillow' of the race.

When Gsell was starting his work in the Northern Territory, the Catholic hierarchy in Australia showed little interest in Aboriginal welfare. It was much more concerned with issues such as the survival of Catholic schools for the European population. Catholics were a large minority in a Protestant Australia. Australia was still technically a 'mission territory' and remained so until 1967. Their mission was to the European Catholics, swamped by often hostile Protestants, not to Aboriginal people.[5]

The Catholic bishops expressed some concern for Aboriginal people in 1885 after a Plenary Council of bishops in Sydney, deploring that they had not been converted to Christianity. European settlers, they lamented, had supposedly both 'corrupted [Aboriginal people's] morals' as they 'enriched themselves'.[6] Given the evils of colonisation, the bishops recommended segregating Aboriginal people from Europeans through missions where they would be instructed in religion as well as 'the rudiments of civilisation'.[7]

Yet the church hierarchy did not actually take responsibility for Aboriginal people's wellbeing. Instead, the bishops expressed their hope that maybe the pope would appoint a religious order to the task. Someone else could do it. Until such missions could support themselves, an annual General Collection in every church in the Australasian Diocese would provide for them. But local congregations were already being called upon to support Catholic schools and churches. They were much less enthusiastic about financially supporting Aboriginal missions. In 1888, Cardinal Moran wrote of the Church's responsibility to 'impart the blessings of civilisation and religion to the Aboriginal races.' Yet, to him, this was a racialised task. The 'Irish race', he thought, was already too busy building churches, convents and schools for the European Catholic population. Aboriginal people were not to be an Irish Catholic responsibility, that work would fall to non–English speaking Europeans.[8]

Gsell and the Missionaries of the Sacred Heart

So it took a German-born Frenchman, Francis Xavier Gsell, and a multilingual, multicultural team to take an interest in the Tiwi. As the Tiwi people emphasise, he came all the way from Europe to work with them; they must have been important:

> In those days when the mission got here, Bishop Gsell, he landed here in 1911. With the boat, you know, all the way from France to us.[9]

> That ship where he was from France to come and visit.[10]

Gsell did not have a high opinion of white Australians: '*ils manquent de patience et de savoir faire avec les sauvages*' ('they lack patience and know-how with the savages').[11] Perhaps he developed this view when he saw how readily the church in Australia passed off Aboriginal mission work to foreign orders. His first team of missionaries at Bathurst Island had no Australians on it. From the beginning, there were the four Filipino crewmen. Later, a brother and a priest joined them. Brother Lambert was German; Father Regis Courbon was French.

But Gsell felt he was missing something – or someone – from his team. Gsell believed that 'a mission without nuns is almost an impossibility; it is like a family without a mother'.[12] He quickly requested that sisters from the Daughters of Our Lady of the Sacred Heart, the MSCs' sister order, join the mission to teach the children and nurse the sick. They were Sister Joseph Schapp, a Dutch woman, and Sister Kieran Doyle, who was Irish.

Back in 1906, Cardinal Moran had applied to the pope, asking him to give responsibility for the Diocese of Darwin to a French missionary society: the Missionaries of the Sacred Heart

(*Missionnaires du Sacré-Coeur*, the MSCs).[13] They were a natural choice; the order had been in Australasia since 1882, when the first band of priests arrived in Sydney in response to the pope's call to evangelise the South Pacific. Their motto – 'may the Sacred Heart of Jesus be everywhere loved' – compelled the French order to reach the furthest parts of the globe. The nuns from Our Lady of the Sacred Heart followed in 1885. Their aim in the Pacific was 'to bring to those who knew not God the blessings of Christian enlightenment and piety'.[14] From Sydney, they went to New Guinea, New Britain and the Gilbert Islands (Kiribati).

Soon after, in 1899, Francis Xavier Gsell arrived in Sydney.[15] Gsell was born in Alsace-Lorraine, then part of Germany, in 1872. His namesake, Francis Xavier, founder of the Jesuits, evangelised South East Asia four centuries before. Perhaps inspired by that saint, Gsell joined the MSCs at age 20, and landed as a missionary in Papua in 1900. His next posting was Palmerston (Darwin) in 1906, running a Catholic school (until nuns arrived) and establishing the parish as Administrator Apostolic of the Diocese of Darwin. His eye, however, was on Aboriginal people and the possibilities of starting a mission. Gsell pondered whether Rome might give him the whole region to evangelise:

> Northern Territory, my large and beautiful province called
> Kimberley … This province is very rich but still scarcely
> populated by white people, there are, however, a lot of blacks …
> The Catholic Fathers have a mission in Beagle Bay, but with the
> exception of the small parish of Broome south of Beagle B. they
> only care for the blacks surrounding their monastery.[16]

The Tiwi Islands seemed ideal for a mission. The surrounding waters are often rough, so it would be easy to keep Tiwi in and 'undesirables' (buffalo shooters, for instance) out. Yet the islands were close enough to Darwin to be easily supplied. Melville Island was not available as an option because it was leased to the buffalo hunters. But Bathurst

Island might fit the bill. With government backing, Gsell envisaged establishing an independent, self-governing Aboriginal community, entirely separated from other whites:

> If it is granted we will have an ideal field for our mission. Certainly there are not many savages there; but once the mission has been organised, we can easily induce the natives of the dry land to settle there, and thus under the protection and with the help of the Government we will be able to organise a sort of [reservation] or an indigenous State separated from the whites and self-sufficient.[17]

Gsell approached the South Australian government to declare Bathurst Island a reserve and allow him to establish a mission. They declined. Gsell put this down to prejudice against missionaries.[18] In 1911, administration of the Northern Territory would be transferred to the Commonwealth Government. So in anticipation in July 1910, he wrote to the Government Resident in Palmerston. Given the 'urgent need' for the 'moral and social betterment of the aboriginal race', he proposed that the Catholic Church do something to help these 'less fortunate brethren out of their degraded state'. This assistance would be in the form of an 'institution' where he would teach agriculture, literacy, religious training and 'all the attainments that would make them useful members of society'. Since institutions such as these had failed on the mainland (he was thinking of the Jesuit mission on the Daly River), he needed a 'large and fertile island'. Bathurst Island would be perfect.[19] The area around the mission was subsequently made an Aboriginal Reserve on 13 March 1912. The whole of Bathurst Island was declared 'Wongoak Aboriginal Reserve' on 12 December 1912. Because it was a reserve, only missionaries and government agents would be permitted to visit. Through this measure, in alliance with Gsell, the Tiwi also succeeded in establishing a limit on who could intrude on their Country, keeping further white invaders out.

Gsell's arrival

Gsell made a quick exploratory visit to Bathurst Island in 1911, guided by a Chinese man, Lee, and a Filipino whose name was unrecorded. Tiwi historians remember the Filipino and they remember there was one Tiwi man who met Gsell's party on the beach.[20] That was Wanamatyuwa, who told them 'Nguiu' was the name of the place where they landed.[21] Other Tiwi accounts say Gsell also met Mulankinya and his wife Julanimawu on the beach. Seeing Gsell across the Apsley Strait, they paddled out from Paru to greet him. After Gsell chose 'Ngooyoo' (Nguiu) to be the site of the future mission, Gsell was led to believe that it was, in fact, ideal in light of local politics. Nguiu, he understood, was a 'no man's land', 'accessible to all without interference'. Gsell put his luck down to 'the guidance of Divine Providence'.[22] But perhaps there were other factors at work. It is likely Tiwi people themselves guided the visitor to the most appropriate place.

Whether the territory was actually 'neutral' is doubtful. We suspect Gsell was misinformed. One woman tells us that Gsell 'just came and helped himself to the land'.[23] Anthropologist Charles Hart described it as 'virtually in Tiklauila [Jikilaruwu] Territory'. This was significant, he claimed, because men from this Country were the first to work as mediators and translators for Gsell. They were his hosts. One, a 25-year-old named Mariano Munkara, 'created something of a monopoly in the job of white man's escort and adviser' and was 'devoted to the cultivation of white men'. His brothers, Louis, Tipperary, and Antonio Munkara were too, though to a lesser degree.[24] Perhaps Mariano felt an obligation to ensure peaceful relations on their Country.

Today, the site of the mission is acknowledged as Mantiyupwi land, with the Jikilaruwu as near neighbours and close relatives.[25] Mulankinya, the first to welcome Gsell, was also a Traditional Owner of the area. But the Tiwi system of land tenure is somewhat flexible, according to political negotiations and spiritual connections.[26] Some

Tiwi emphasise Gsell's declaration that this was everyone's Country now, so it should be shared.[27] But the Mantiyupwi hold responsibility for that Country, even though they welcome others who now also live there.

Tiwi people also remember the father of those four entrepreneurial brothers, Antonio, Mariano, Louis and Tipperary. Their father, Old Turimpi, was an important cultural broker. He is credited with the oversight of his sons' work and, ultimately of Gsell himself. It is not clear exactly when Turimpi died. Hart claims he was already dead when Gsell arrived. Tiwi people tell a story of Old Turimpi living in Darwin. At night, in the darkness, he saw the lights of the very first motor car in Darwin approaching. To him, they were the min min lights, a devil, in the dark. Petrified, the old man had a fatal heart attack. He is buried down at Mindil Beach, under the casino. Tiwi people still sing the song about Old Turimpi and his fate. It is a song about modernity and change. Despite all the work Turimpi did guiding his people into this new stage of their history, he did not see the dangers to come. The ramifications are ominous.

Returning to Gsell, during that first night, Gsell's camp awoke to sounds of girls screaming and discovered two Iwaidja men who worked for Cooper, armed with rifles, trying to smuggle two 'stolen' Tiwi girls across the strait. Gsell's ideas about the plight of Tiwi women formed early.[28]

On 1 June 1911, a team of five missionaries set out from Port Darwin to Nguiu to establish the mission. They were Gsell and four other Catholic men, all Filipinos. Gsell needed people with sailing skills to guide him. He found four Filipino pearlers in Darwin who knew the waters, knew his god and believed in his mission. He paid them 'a few shillings', fed and clothed them.[29] Though these four missionary pioneers were integral to Gsell's success, Gsell never named them in his writings; such were the racial politics of North Australia and missionary work. One of them was probably Alphonso, another Matthew Garr. We do not know the names of the others.

The five pulled up on the beach that evening. There was no one there. In his memoir, Gsell explained that the absence of Tiwi people was because they were in hiding on the mistaken belief that Gsell's party were police, come to intervene in disputes between the Tiwi and the Iwaidja.[30]

Tiwi histories of Gsell's coming

For Tiwi, the crucial part of the story is their decision to come in and find out about the missionary. They were curious. Gsell convinced them to come to him in an unlikely way. He found something that would pique their interest and attention. He gave them his glasses.

> They thought it was a ghost. So he showed them the glass. This story was told by the Old People. He gave them the glass to go to every country where they stayed. And told them about the missionary, about himself. So they all came when they saw that the message came.[31]

The Tiwi were not the only Aboriginal people to 'see' white intruders as ghosts. One Nyoongar woman in 1841 even insisted the explorer George Grey was the ghost of her dead son. 'Recognising' white people as ghosts pointed to their strangeness, and to their danger.[32] Gsell never recorded this incident. It's not even clear that he knew that the glasses were so attractive to Tiwi people. But the Tiwi remember. Perhaps without realising it, he was re-enacting an earlier 'first contact' gesture; Arthur Phillip gave a looking glass to an Aboriginal man at Botany Bay in January 1788. When Gsell arrived, he gave his glasses to a Tiwi man (or men) with instructions, 'take this glass to Tikalaru, Rangku, Malau', that is, all over Bathurst Island, 'and show the Tiwi people'.[33] The glasses, for the Tiwi, somehow contained the message that they must come to see this white man. Another woman, Dulcie Kelantumama, told the story in detail:

It was like, about that patuma, we call it eye glasses, patuma, the eye glass name in English, patuma is eye glass. We got it on for our eyes to look. Those two people Molungina and Tuluamamo happened, they probably knew something about that white man was here too. He only came when they came all the way, they came all the way down here where Bishop Gsell was. And I can't tell you much about them how they approach him or how they came to him, but I heard a story about that he gave them the eyeglass, his eyeglass, one of his, maybe his old eyeglass. And he gave those two people to take it round to all the places around Tiwi island. Take it to Tikalaru, Malau, Rangku, Munupi Garden Point right around to Tumalumpi and to Tumalumpi across by boat. That's how the glasses came and all those people heard about it.

They was surprised to see a glass. Which told the Tiwi people in those days that such a thing like that is not anywhere around the Tiwi islands, to them it was a big surprise.

And then they said to themselves, 'must be a muruntani, a white man, living on the island, came to the island. We'll have to go'. That's how the glasses told them that they had to come and find out for themselves if he really was here. And they did, and they all came, they all found the white man.[34]

Some say it was Mulankinya who went around with the glasses. In another version of the story, told by Romolo Kantilla, the glasses were given to a Tiwi man who remained at the beach, while Gsell himself travelled around the islands.[35] In this account, the Tiwi and the missionary used the glasses as an exercise in proving mutual trust. When Gsell returned to find the old man, who had remained at the beach with the glasses and guided him with the big smoke, he rewarded him with material goods and spiritual knowledge. The old man, in return, invited his kin to come to the mission. Other narrators emphasised the way that the glasses fascinated the Tiwi and convinced them that they must come to the missionary:

> That's when all the people come in because of the glass, reading glass. Or sunglass maybe! This when they go see, first time in their life they've seen it and they were all happy. They didn't make fuss about it.[36]

It's not that the message 'came with the glasses'. No, the glasses, 'it was the message'.[37] The glasses became a kind of message stick, summoning Tiwi to the beach with the missionary, just as message sticks would go around for important ceremonial events. Some Tiwi historians say Gsell himself sent a message stick:

> And he was like, he told them, 'Come here'. I want you to go and tell everyone to come down. I've got something to give to, to people. So, he just sent a message stick asking to everyone 'come and look'.[38]

Some say it was not looking glasses but a magnifying glass that went around. Either way, Gsell was working within an existing Tiwi cultural practice of sending messages around using special objects. Perhaps by giving this valuable object to the Tiwi, telling them to take it across their Country, Gsell demonstrated his trust in them and generous disposition towards them. And the white man's willingness to part with this curious object signalled his willingness to share other goods.

As another woman explained, there's 'something meaning about that glass', 'it's like light to see'.[39] This was not just any object. Anthropologist Francesca Merlan found that all over Australia, Aboriginal people took an early interest in luminescent objects: bottles, pearl shells, beads, glass. These were what they wanted most from colonisers. They seem to have been given 'special regard', even 'sacredness' in Aboriginal systems of meaning.[40] Glass has incredible properties and deep symbolic meaning in many cultures. It improves sight but can also be seen past or through; missionaries the world over used mirrors, glass and light as metaphors. Whereas 'heathens' were 'blind', with the light of Christ, they would 'see'. Missionaries bore the 'light', hoping people would see the likeness of Christ in themselves, the faithful reflection.[41]

So the story of the glasses is a story about knowing, recognising, seeing. For generations of Tiwi familiar with Catholic tradition, the story also echoes Biblical narratives of the calling of disciples, but with the Tiwi showing that they are really the ones with 'ears to hear' and 'eyes to see'. Tiwi histories focus on the Tiwi eagerness to embrace the new, rather than the wisdom or virtue of the missionaries. These are stories about Tiwi insight. Perhaps the Tiwi 'saw through' the missionaries, like glass, understanding they were not always as they seemed, but that they could also give the Tiwi new forms of insight:

> Lucky he didn't get spear when he was on the beach, he brought flour, he brought calico, tobacco, sugar. He brought them everything. And a mirror, so they can look at themself.[42]

Once Tiwi people encountered Gsell, there were other reasons to remain in contact. He 'brought them everything'. He had tobacco, sugar, tea, flour, and as Tiwi historian Bernard Tipiloura emphasised, it was 'free':

> Well, because I born in the bush and then when my parents heard, 'Oh, there's a good missionary'. So what happened, we have to go there, because he giving out free tobacco … Free tobacco and free flour. Yeah, free sugar and tea.[43]

Gsell's offerings of both material goods and new spiritual insights distinguished him from other white visitors. It is possible the Tiwi knew a little about missionaries and Christianity from their

Iwaidja neighbours' experiences with Confalonieri (though this was generations earlier) or the stories of the Jesuits on the Daly River not long before. Whatever they knew or did not know about missionaries, they could see Gsell was different to the buffalo hunters:

It was different, because he was a different priest come along, and he was telling them about God ... He was telling about Jesus, and he told them, you are walking in his land, you're drinking water, he's a person that make this earth for you mob to live, bush tucker, he gave you bush tucker. He gave you the culture, see, Tiwi culture, all that. Yes, and after, that's what, he baptised 200 a day, baptised to be Christian.[44]

Teddy Portaminni explained how Gsell told the Tiwi of his mission from God. But at first, the Tiwi really just wanted to know what he had for them:

[Gsell] said, 'No, I'm from up there. That man up there. He sent me here, to you people'. 'So, I can help you ... be civilised people, you know.' 'What are you going to give us?' So, he said, 'Oh yeah, alright. Came out [gave] them biscuits, you want tobacco'. 'Hey, this is good. I will stay here with you.' So, he set up a mission here.[45]

The glass, the goods and the knowledge gave Tiwi people confidence and reason to visit the mission, even leave their children at the station, but they did not induce them to settle permanently. Instead, they came and went from their Country, visiting the mission as necessary. Only two men stayed with Gsell at first: Boolack and Tokoopa. After a week those two, together with the four Filipinos and Gsell, had built a temporary chapel with a storeroom and bedroom. Gsell said the first mass that week on the Feast of the Sacred Heart. Gradually, over the months, more men came in.[46] Together, they built the kitchen, school and church, and received food and tobacco for their labour. One Tiwi woman spoke proudly of her father's construction work:

> They used to cut the log, you know. Timber, to build that church, old church. Old one church. My father is one of them, my own father. I was like that [indicates, small]. Four five, six men, six or seven men, eight, built the church.[47]

Before people came down to the mission, they had a special ceremony to mark the occasion. They sang songs about getting new things from the mission and putting on European clothes. Today, the history of coming down to the mission is memorialised through that song. It is sung today in ceremony. But the song about putting on clothes, for the first time, is bittersweet. It is about Tiwi ways of being a modern people, leaving the old and embracing the new: the relentlessness of change, and Tiwi resilience through it all.

The establishment of the mission

Gsell called the mission station 'St Francis Xavier', not quite named after himself, but very close.[48] It's possible his Filipino co-workers suggested using the name of the first missionary to their own people, Francis Xavier. Gsell named the church St Therese after the 'Little Flower', Marie Françoise-Thérèse Martin of Lisieux. St Therese later also became the name of the school on Bathurst Island. Eventually, 'Francis Xavier' was dropped and the whole mission became known as St Therese's Mission. The missionaries thought this name was 'more modern' but also thought it fitted the missions' focus on children, especially girls.[49] Therese and variants are now common names on the Tiwi Islands. Her feast day is still celebrated in Wurrumiyanga.

Thérèse was a young French Carmelite nun, born only a few months after Gsell, but died in 1897, aged 24, of tuberculosis. She became famous for her writings on the 'little way', the 'way of spiritual

Bathurst Island children, nuns and horses, no date.
MSC Archives Kensington

childhood' and was canonised in 1925.[50] She taught, especially, the value of child-like innocence and, in one passage, described the 'poor savages' of the world as 'wild flowers', beautiful to God for their humble status and simple lives. For her, Indigenous peoples were just like children.[51]

*

Gsell sometimes used the same language when he wrote about the Tiwi. Aboriginal people were 'bush children' or 'overgrown children' and the Tiwi were 'big children'.[52] His understanding fit with a common white view at the time that Aboriginal people were somehow a 'child race'. Perhaps in honouring St Thérèse, Gsell signalled his belief in the worth of Tiwi, precisely in (what he perceived) to be their humble status. Needless to say, this is not how Tiwi viewed their situation. In creating a reserve, intending to isolate Tiwi from supposed corrupting influences, Gsell designed to preserve what he saw as their innocence, like a Edenic garden. His later focus on little girls – 'flowers' – and their purity and piety in domestic convent life further signalled the mission's concern for all things small and simple, and for keeping Tiwi people this way.

Tiwi could not have known the full meaning of Gsell's intentions at this early stage. Gsell worked hard to appear respectful. His objective was to win the trust of the Tiwi. He considered the role of the missionary in the early years to be simply to 'give a willing helping hand', to 'be cheerful' because Aboriginal people are 'big children, they like to play and laugh'. 'If you make them feel you are here to serve their needs, they will give in, they become friendly & trust you. Never play the boss.'[53]

So Gsell did not attempt to change Tiwi beliefs or culture at first. According to Gsell, he waited ten years before trying to teach the Gospel because of the language barrier. According to Tiwi people, '[the missionaries] didn't come and blend in with their culture. He took ten years for the priest [Gsell] to understand about our culture'.[54] From both perspectives, the first decade (at least) was marked by mutual misunderstanding and shallow communication.

Though he did not preach or teach, Gsell still believed he could travel the 'road to the soul' 'through the body'. So he also turned to medical services to win the trust of the Tiwi. The mission's methods were rudimentary. They had Epsom salts, castor oil, aspirin, tincture of iodine, vaseline and smelling salts. With only a book, some 'lessons from a Darwin dentist' and 'a full set of forceps' ('instruments of torture', he called them), 'thus armed', Gsell began offering dentistry. Although these remedies were basic, Gsell found them effective, both for curing disease and as an 'entrance into the heart of my black friends'.[55]

The terrible sickness

Despite the mission's medical interventions, in February 1913, nearly a third of the Tiwi died in only two weeks. The epidemic began at Christmas time, 1912. Tiwi from all over the islands came into the mission, probably for Christmas celebrations. Government medical inspector Henry Fry went to the islands to investigate and found that, of a population of 650 people, 187 had died.[56] He listened to the old man, Korupu, singing a song about the sickness: 'magic starts with feeling like snake walking up legs, the stomach and bloody diarrhoea, when reaches heart, no more eat, die'.[57]

The symptoms Korupu described were consistent with poisoning, but white experts thought it might be measles.[58] This would make sense in a population hitherto isolated from the disease. Perhaps the missionaries had brought it. Fiji and Hawai'i experienced similar epidemics after contact with white populations for the first time. In Hawai'i, observers noted that children of missionaries were unaffected; they were immune. The Tiwi song about 'stomach and bloody diarrhoea' matches the gastrointestinal problems which were the major cause of death among Fijians first exposed to measles.[59] But Fry had his doubts. If it were measles, why were Tiwi children relatively unaffected? No, 'the extremely low number of infant deaths was entirely against measles being the cause of the holocaust, and supports the native diagnosis of magic'.[60]

Another theory, put forward by anthropologist Eric Venbrux, is that the brackish water of the creek at the mission was 'poisoned'. This would not have affected missionaries; they drank from their own well. Venbrux found that Tiwi employed their own spiritual power through the kulama yam ceremony and the jamparipari Dreaming to combat the poison.[61] In 1954, the anthropologist Jane Goodale asked Korupu about the cause of the epidemic. It was still fresh in his memory. The white people had brought mainlanders (Iwaidja people) over. They were the ones who brought over mainland magic and sang poison songs. The magic in the songs caused the deaths.[62]

If so, the fact that the missionaries were unscathed could only confirm the missionary power over this mainland magic. But why would the Iwaidja have poisoned the Tiwi? Perhaps they saw that the Tiwi, now, had found their own white patrons, with their own access to tobacco, flour, and potentially guns. Venbrux also noticed the epidemic was a 'watershed' in Tiwi history. It marked the end of the long Tiwi resistance to the intrusion of outsiders and the beginning of a new approach to the outside world.[63] Everything changed after that.

Not long after the deaths, the Tiwi got rid of Joe Cooper and his Iwaidja men. This time, rather than their sneak attack strategy as in the past, Tiwi people made their move via their powerful white man. They used their missionary against him:

> Well, he had a bit of trouble too, Joe Cooper from them, from the Tiwi man, Tiwi people, because they were not good, some of the people from the Iwaidja. He didn't actually do a good thing … The priest [Gsell] and him had some, or the two men had some talk or meeting and, 'You've got to tell your [Iwaidja] men that. Stop him. Stop them from humbugging to the women because they belong to the Tiwi men.'[64]

> You know what I heard that bishop he told [Joe Cooper] to leave, the bishop Gsell, he told him to leave, he went across and he said, 'You've got to start to leave, you better go', so he went back to mainland. But that's the history about Joe Cooper, he was a really bad person, he wasn't a good person. And the bishop, that bishop came and he baptised everyone, he gave them, opened up the new store where they provide flour, teabags, sugar, and black tobacco, niki niki.[65]

Gsell exorcised their Country of the Iwaidja magic and sent them away. After that, the Tiwi had their own source of baptism (and spiritual power), and their own supply of flour, tea, sugar and tobacco. According to the government archives, Gsell's assistant, the missionary priest, Father Courbon, along with Sam Green recommended that Cooper and all the mainlanders be deported and the 'stolen' women returned. Eventually, the Northern Territory Administration ordered Cooper and his workers to leave the island in late 1915. Some of the 'stolen' Tiwi women wanted to stay with their husbands and go with them to the mainland. They were not allowed to, although Gsell believed that some did anyway. For the priests, this was their first act of 'protecting' Tiwi women. Later, Jane Goodale learned that the Jikilaruwu band (that is, the sons of Turimpi: Louis, his brothers and kin) turned to the missionaries when they were unable to form an alliance with Joe Cooper themselves.[66] Various Aboriginal groups jostled for the favour of white newcomers. Now the Tiwi had found a white patron: a newcomer they saw as rich with material wealth, political and spiritual power.

But at this stage, the missionaries still had little influence over Tiwi people's day-to-day lives. The Tiwi still came and went from the mission as they pleased. That began to change when a young girl, Martina, chose to use the missionaries as leverage for important marriage reform. Tiwi girls wanted more options, and the mission became a way to get them.

7

SHE STARTED IT

Dulcie Kelantumama

Martina, she's my grandmother. This is all I know about her. They didn't have this place, it was all bushy. That was when Bishop Gsell or Father Gsell, they called him bishop at that time, in 1911, he came to Nguiu.

He set a camp for himself, that's the place where he was. Grandma came along. You probably heard about him going around where they lived, homelands, you know, Aboriginal camps.

My grandmother happened to come from Malau. From there, she was about twelve or thirteen years of age, she was young, when an old man asked her for marriage. A young girl in those days would join an old man, would go along and camp with him. But I don't know what happened to my grandmother, she fled. She ran away.

She didn't want him. She didn't want to be the youngest wife for him. He had other wives already and he wanted her to be his youngest wife. Maybe in the night-time, I don't know what time that was when she ran from that place and come to Garden Point on the other side. I was thinking she must have found a canoe or something. I don't know how many kilometres it is from Malau to that end. But she did. The way I heard those people in the past saying, 'she swam, there was a big creek'. 'How can she swim?' I was thinking. I'm thinking they must have gotten a little canoe, paddle along. She maybe got a canoe.

At the end of that beach here she got on the shore. She went up to that little settlement the bishop make, she went up to him and he saw her. I think she didn't tell him herself that she was afraid of him with the colour. She probably was afraid. I don't know what made her go ahead and meet the white man. Maybe he had courage about how you do God's work and all that. And he invited her along in the settlement he built.

She was with the bishop, bishop or father. And then the next day there was another canoe came along with a group of them. That man who hunted for her and he had some men with him, a few of the tribal, you know. They came behind and they all went to that place, where father was. And as he saw them, he must have prayed to the Lord or something like that to bring himself peace with the warriors, you know. They came with spears. And when they stood in front of him and he saw them, I think he made peace with them.

And all of a sudden, he traded some of the things that he had, because in those days Tiwi people had never seen anything like that. He got them flour, tobacco, he gave them that, or maybe a round tobacco to smoke. Everything was new to them and they all felt, all of a sudden they felt good and happy because something new had reached them.

That father brought some new things with him. And they had never seen it. When you live out in the bush you don't know the white man, you don't know those things. And he sold them. And they all wanted a mirror or something like that, glass. His glass, he sold them that, and then they all were all very excited about the new things that have come to them, they have never seen it. And then they went back, they went back to their community where they came from, Malau.

She didn't want to be the last wife or the youngest wife or that because she was so very young, and he had all the other wives with him. So she probably ran away for that reason you know. She had the courage to do that, run away, and change everything. And when she first came to the bishop she had only one and then a few more came from the bush. Few more ladies came along.

It's just like now God send that man here to grab hold of the people. Tiwi people, grab all of them, and start teaching them about Catholic faith. Baptism, he baptised them. My grandmother was the first one then all of them they heard the news, you know. They send each other the news on the letter stick. The news about the old man came: 'white man, he's here'. I don't know what name they named this place but tell them, tell them he's here. And everyone started to come this way. All of them from that other side coming this way. And in the end we are all here.

But it is a pity I didn't grow up with my grandmother. Growing up I wasn't with my grandmother. She died at East Arm with that leprosy sickness. Some of them were out at East Arm Settlement in Darwin.

That's how we're all here today. That's why I thank my grandmother for doing an event like that, for running away. My grandmother, she started it.

8

THE GIRL WHO TURNED HER WORLD AROUND

Laura Rademaker
& Mavis Kerinaiua

A Topsy doll is one that flips upside down. Turn her over and, instead of legs beneath her skirt, she has an alter ego. These dolls are usually female, with a black girl on one end and a white girl on the other. They came from the American South in the 19th century, but gained global popularity even as far as Australia, and were sold and made in Australia from at least the early 20th century.

When Ungaraminingamo, a teenaged Tiwi girl, met the French missionary on the beach on the Tiwi Islands in North Australia, he gave her the English name 'Topsy', like the doll. It was common for settlers to give this name to Aboriginal women at the time. Later, in 1928, the missionary baptised her and she became Martina, in honour of St Therese Martin, the 'little flower'.[1] Martina was the first of the '150 wives'.

Missionaries and their supporters celebrated 'Topsy' as their first Catholic convert, and considered her one of the first fruits of Gsell's 'going native' strategy. In his memoir *The Bishop with 150 Wives*, Gsell depicted a topsy-turvy world where a priest might become a polygamist and a 'native' become a Catholic. The story was meant to charm, thanks to the extreme difference between himself – the white, male, Catholic – and the Tiwi woman, black and 'pagan'. But,

Tiwi girls, Bishop Gsell and nuns, no date.
MSC Archives, Kensington

as Tiwi historians tell the story, it was actually Ungaraminingamo who turned the world around.

Although she became Martina (and the Tiwi remember her by that name), we want to tell how she was also Topsy. Like the Topsy doll, she was a woman for whom things are not as they seem. According to Tiwi, *she* was the one who turned everything upside down, in order to make big changes for Tiwi women.

'Wives' for 'sale'

But first, why did Gsell even think that he could 'buy' women from the Tiwi? How could such a trade be appropriate for a priest? Some contemporary missionaries found the idea repulsive. On the Anglican mission at Oenpelli (Gunbalanya), the superintendent claimed in 1928 that there were 'large numbers of blacks about &

children, whom they want to sell but I am not buying'.[2] Leaving aside the question of whether Bininj people really did intend to 'sell' their children (they probably expected some kind of gift exchange, but 'selling' is doubtful), this missionary was appalled by what he thought was a traffic in children.

Still, not everyone agreed. Another Anglican missionary, just over a decade later, began compensating men for giving up their wives on Groote Eylandt in the Gulf of Carpentaria. By the 1950s, that mission had a formal system for the transaction, with a fixed rate per woman and a proforma contract for men to sign.[3] For missionaries, this was about eliminating polygamy. They also thought that the way these marriage customs created interdependence across generations got in the way of missionaries converting the youth; they wanted to separate old from young, thinking they could have greater influence over the young. At the Roper River mission (Ngukurr) as early as 1915, one Presbyterian missionary described Anglican missionaries as attempting 'buying of the girls from the old men' to redistribute wives to younger men and found it 'a very satisfactory method'.[4] So Gsell may not even have come up with the idea himself. According to historian Regina Ganter, the Jesuit missionaries at Daly River had experimented with 'buying' girls in the 1880s and 1890s.[5] Exchanging gifts for girls was a potential strategy for missionaries who wanted to change Aboriginal family life, whether they went so far as to call it a 'purchase' or not.

According to the priest's records, Gsell began accumulating girls in 1916, starting with Martina. By 1918, there were 40 children in his dormitory (referred to as an 'orphanage', even though the children had family), receiving schooling in the 'four Rs': reading, writing, arithmetic and religious instruction.[6] Gsell first publicly mentioned his 'buying' of children in the *Catholic Press* in 1918 but notably did not suggest this was exclusively girls, nor anything to do with rescuing them from a supposedly oppressive Tiwi marriage system. It was all about access to the young:

Our main action is with the children; and, in order to be able to keep them on the station, we have to buy them from the parents, as otherwise they interfere too much with them, and impose on them their own pagan customs. It will be an expensive means, but the only efficacious one.[7]

This might be surprising, given that the idea that Tiwi girls were supposedly 'chattel' to greedy geriatrics was so central to Gsell's later account in *The Bishop with 150 Wives*. His failure to mention slavery from the outset suggests, perhaps, that this explanation came later, that it was retrofitted as an explanation for a practice that was already convenient for the mission. The idea of saving Tiwi girls certainly piqued the public imagination and brought publicity to the mission. This is not to say that Gsell did not think Tiwi marriage was oppressive. He did. Only that it was not, at first, his main concern. And this is not surprising. You see, the Tiwi do not mention slavery in their histories either. Tiwi women wanted marriage reform and used Gsell's belief that he was 'buying' women to achieve it, but their objectives were quite different to the missionaries'.

Setting the record straight

Martina is an important figure to the Tiwi people, especially Tiwi women on Bathurst Island. She was the one who established their biggest town, Wurrumiyanga. Before Martina, 'they didn't have this place, it was all bushy'. Martina was a leader among women, the first to open new ways and new opportunities for her younger sisters and daughters. 'She had the courage to do that, run away, and change everything'.[8]

Tiwi histories of the so-called '150 wives' are not like Gsell's. Although Tiwi people learned the story from their Old People, they also learned it from the missionaries. Not many have read Gsell's book, but his version of the story circulated in their community, via the priests and nuns, and was often retold in their Catholic school. Even though they know Gsell's version, the Tiwi history is strikingly, deliberately different. For example, according to Tiwi historians, Martina objected, not to the Tiwi marriage system itself, but to her particular situation:

> She was promised to the old man. I think she didn't like, she didn't like that one. That's the way, you know, we have promises … She was scared too because he was really old man. She was young.[9]

Before the mission, a Tiwi household or camp was made up of a man, his wives, their children and sons-in-law, and any others who might be dependent on the group. Everyone had a role, and the young generally worked to provide for their elders. Men and women hunted for animals and shellfish. Men also hunted birds and fish. Women provided roots, vegetables and fruit. A woman was promised to her first husband before she was born. This was because a woman gained her son-in-law at puberty. Any daughters she would have in the future would be promised to that man. Her son-in-law would be around her own age – about thirty years old – by the time he received his first wife. This man would give gifts to his mother-in-law and show her special respect. He would live with his mother-in-law's household, hunting for her and giving her gifts. The son-in-law and mother-in-law were called *ambrinua*. Since they were the same age, this relationship lasted their whole life.[10]

When a girl was nearing puberty, her father took her to her husband's fireplace and told her to sleep at his side. This man, her first husband, was in charge of her education. He was like a father figure. When her first period arrived, she went through the *muringaleta* ceremony. She was now a woman and became a mother-in-law.[11]

According to some accounts, Martina was the thirteenth wife to the old man Merapanui.[12] Others say it was more like number four. Either way, it was a difficult position. The youngest wife had the least

74

power in a Tiwi household. The eldest had likely had many husbands before, since she was first married as a young girl. Now it was her turn to be matriarch. She controlled everything. The eldest wife was the boss, responsible for the provision of food and assigning daily work to younger men and women. She directed them where and when to gather food and what they should seek out. She instructed younger mothers. She told younger wives to gather firewood and collect water. Often, her husband would be considerably younger than her too. His responsibilities would tend to be more political and religious. Her responsibilities were economic; she was the provider, so, naturally, she could be bossy. As one Tiwi woman explained in the 1950s, 'she can sit all day in a camp and send the other wives out hunting'.[13] As the youngest, Martina could be left to do the chores while older or favoured women did nothing. Tiwi women explained Martina's objections to becoming Merapanui's youngest wife:

> She run away, she didn't want to live with that old man, promised, engaged. Our law, not to break the promise. It was our law. The old men promised to three, four women those days. He could send one hunting, one clean up, one takem. Men used to, that woman used to stay, that husband one girl, other girl, other one hunting, two wives. Favourite spending time with her out bush and the other doing all the cleaning.[14]

Francillia Puruntatameri, an emerging Tiwi historian, was told that even Martina's own family had concerns about Martina's status and treatment as the youngest wife to Merapanui:

> She was number four. He wanted her to be the fourth wife, but the family said no, her Dad said no, you go. Already he's got all her sisters. Merapanui was married to her three older sisters, and she didn't want to be number four. From the same mother. Their mother is tribe of pandanus, but their father's tribe is the rock, from Rocky Point.[15]

There was another category of wife in Tiwi law: the ningyka ('chosen one'). A man could bestow this role on a girl when she was first brought to his camp. She would always begin as the youngest wife. As ningyka, she must follow him constantly. She could only eat food he gave her. Most importantly, she could not have other lovers (as her co-wives could). Only a virgin could become ningyka and they were expected to have their first sexual experiences with their husband. It was not an attractive option for young women; most young women thought the lives of ningyka were too restricted.[16] The ningyka experience resonates with Martina's:

> She was about twelve or thirteen years of age, she was young when a old man asked her for marriage … She didn't want to be the youngest wife for him. He had other wives already and he wanted her to be his youngest wife.[17]

Perhaps Martina was a ningyka; the old man was her first husband. 'She didn't want him', one of her granddaughters said. Tiwi historians emphasise that she was so young and her husband was so old. They say she was only thirteen. The priest's records claim she was sixteen. Either way, her muringaleta ceremony had only recently occurred. 'She was so very young and he had all the other wives with him.' There were suggestions that he had singled her out for special, unwanted attention. He did not simply want her as a wife, he 'wanted her to be his youngest wife'.[18] Martina did not like to spend so much time with him. By the 1950s, Tiwi understood that those at the mission who lived as monogamous couples were 'like ningyka'. Ningyka-style living (that is, monogamy) became associated with the mission and its teaching. It is likely that Martina herself began this association between the mission and ningyka marriage, as she was eventually the first to be married at the mission.

The only way women could release themselves from an unwanted ningyka situation was by taking a lover.[19] She would need to run and find another man. And this is what Martina did. 'She ran from that place'.[20] The catalyst, it seems, was a particularly nasty argument with her husband.[21] Martina's granddaughter tells how Martina travelled across the landscape and down the Apsley Strait to the beach. She went along the road, to the other end of her Country, to Garden Point and then down. Just as the journeys of the Creative Beings, long ago, formed the Country, Martina's journey across the landscape is an important element of the story of how the township of today was formed on its site. The Old People used to say that 'she swam, there was a big creek'. She went so far she must have taken 'a little canoe, paddle along, she maybe got a canoe'.[22]

And her family was supportive. Francillia Puruntatameri even reported that Martina's father encouraged her to run: 'Martina's dad. He didn't want her to marry to her promise. That's why he sent her out to a mission, he sent his daughter here to the mission to be baptised'.[23] Martina was not breaking the rules of Tiwi culture at all; she was well within her rights as a Tiwi woman to leave.

She arrived at the beach and met the priest. Her husband and his brothers came after her:

> And then maybe the next day there was another canoe came
> along with a group of them. That man who hunted for her
> and he had some men with him, a few of the tribal, you know.
> They came behind and they all went to that place, where Father
> [Gsell] was.[24]

Martina had been speared in the leg at some stage while making her getaway:

> She jump on that canoe, [Merapanui] threw that spear and she
> was hurt. She was speared. She kept on going, going, going,
> going. She made it, she came here.[25]

> But they saw that she left the camp and they followed her. They
> came down. They came down and then they saw. And then a

spear flew and hit her on the leg. Then she came with the spear on the leg where the bishop was.[26]

It was not unusual for women to 'run' from their husbands in Tiwi culture. There was a whole ceremonial tradition around it. The muringaleta ceremony involved a ritual running away from a girl's husband. She would run slowly, to make sure he caught her. Women actually had considerable freedom to choose their partner as they always had the option of leaving their husbands. If a woman left, men had to renegotiate their arrangements. So a husband who wanted to keep his wife would have to treat her well. It was also quite normal for a wife to have a boyfriend as well as a husband. If a wife left, her husband was not to take physical action against her, but against the lover and his kin. So when the old man speared Martina in the leg, he was acting inappropriately by Tiwi law. In these disputes, the woman was always able to stay with her new husband. Any battle was not so much about retrieving her than about restoring the honour of the offended man. After the fight, everyone must forget about the trouble, the Tiwi insisted.[27] So the men who went to fight Gsell (who had acted like a lover in letting Martina camp with him), most likely never intended to take Martina back.

Martina had plenty to gain from running. We know from Gsell's account that she had already received her ambrinua (given to her at puberty, not as a baby as Gsell suggested). As son-in-law, he was obligated to provide her with gifts and food for the rest of her life. Gsell misjudged the Tiwi marriage system, thinking that wealth accrued to men by accumulating wives. What he failed to acknowledge was that women, too, gained wealth through their ambrinua and that, for Martina, this relationship was still intact.[28]

In the years following Martina's escape from her marriage and refuge with Gsell, Tiwi men would bring their promised wife to the dormitory and receive gifts from Gsell (what he called 'buying' the girl, though the Tiwi never use that term) in the form of tobacco or flour. The men would be baptised, as the mission required, and marry the girl once she had grown.[29] In the dormitory, nuns were in charge (and we will learn more of their relationship with the girls in the next chapter). Promised husbands were permitted to visit their betrothed in the dormitory, but under the nuns' strict supervision. Girls in the mission dormitory continued to receive gifts from both their ambrinua and their promised husbands, which they could then share with their families. Families would receive this wealth in addition to the 'payment' they received from the missionaries for allowing their daughter to live in the convent. The mission became an economic hub. The dormitory was not entirely a prison either. Although girls were shut in at night, on weekends they went bush, camping with their families (who otherwise camped on the beach nearby). For the mission, this was in part to save on food expenses but was also with a view to keeping Tiwi traditional bush culture alive in some form.

Although the mission sought to discipline and reform Tiwi girls into a model of Catholic domesticity, it actually inadvertently transposed and complemented existing systems of gift-giving around Tiwi marriage. Tiwi people found that the missionaries' system of dormitories could be made into a useful compromise within their own marriage culture. Men could marry younger than they otherwise would, provided they got baptised.[30] Girls had the advantage of delaying motherhood and gaining new knowledge through mission education. Parents were often happy for their children to learn English.[31] Meanwhile, the dormitory functioned to control girls' sexuality and protect the claims of promised husbands from potential rivals (teenage girls, attractive and unencumbered by children, were the most likely of all women to run off with lovers).[32] Despite all the missionary teaching, secret polygamy continued. Many men had one wife at the mission and another in the bush. The missionaries knew about this but chose to ignore it.[33] They were more interested in reforming women's rather than men's sexuality. Of course, the girls bore the cost of this arrangement, being confined to the dormitory. We will be hearing more from them soon.

When Martina's relatives came to fight Gsell, according to Tiwi memory, they were convinced not to attack for two reasons: one spiritual and one material. They noticed a sense of peace which, somehow, calmed them, and Gsell was also offering useful goods.[34] Another Tiwi historian suggests that Joe Cooper gave Gsell the idea to share his possessions to pacify the warriors. Merapanui came to the mission threatening, 'if you don't hand over that girl I'll burn the mission'. Cooper advised Gsell, 'you've got to give them something … You've got to give something to the Tiwi tribe'.[35] Again, this Tiwi historian did not mention anyone 'purchasing' or 'buying' Martina. Gsell was simply to give gifts to smooth over the trouble.

Once the men saw the wealth the priest could provide, they all started to come in. Other girls copied Martina, leaving unwanted marriages for dormitory life: 'a few more came from the bush, few more ladies come along'. The message stick went around, then 'the news about the old man came, "white man, he's here" … and everybody started to come this way. And, in the end, we are all here'.[36]

This story is also about the advent of modernity. 'Everybody wanted to know the new technology … So a lot of people started coming to Father Gsell like he was a shop'.[37] One woman went into detail about Gsell's gifts, demonstrating the possibilities they brought:

And then he showed them how to use a tomahawk. 'Oh, that's a good method for us to use', maybe they said. Then they showed them how to chop the tree, 'oh!', they want like that! 'That's better one, that's better one! That's better than the ones we got now!' And then mirror. They looked themself in the mirror. And then they said to that old bishop, 'you take this woman and we take all the stuff'.[38]

Dulcie Kelantumama emphasised the role of the divine when she told the story. The Lord made peace with the warriors. Martina's decision to run away was part of a divine plan: 'I don't know what

Loading the *Margaret Mary*
MSC Archives Kensington

made her go ahead and meet the white man. Maybe he had courage about, you know, about how you do God's work and all that'.[39] God had sent Gsell, she claimed, and Martina was the first evangelist. The message stick, long used for communication in Aboriginal traditions, quickly became an instrument of evangelism. Its use indicates, for Tiwi historians, the ready harmony between Catholicism and Tiwi traditions:

> God bin send that man here to grab hold of the people. Tiwi people, grab all of them and start teaching them about Catholic faith. Baptism, he baptized them. My grandmother was the first one then all of them they heard the news, you know. They send each other the news on the letter stick. [40]

Another woman explained the story as one of a strong Tiwi woman kneeling to receive the Christian faith:

> [Gsell] brought that first Bible and Christian faith. And this lady [Martina], a really strong lady, she saw the promised husband, she went away from him. She was brave … She found the bishop down the beach and she knelt before him. She said, 'help me! I need some help'. That's brave story of her, brave, brave woman.[41]

These stories also emphasise Tiwi women's important community role through their faith. Around the world, Catholicism has been a way for Indigenous women to increase their social status and challenge social norms.[42] Now, the story of Martina demonstrates to other Tiwi people that God works through strong Tiwi women and reminds the community of women's important roles in the town of Wurrumiyanga. The mission, from which their town grew, was built on the courage of a woman, favoured by God, who brought modernity to the Tiwi people. The women who tell this story position themselves as guardians of this tradition: a modern, Catholic, matriarchal Tiwi society.

Scared because he was white

Tiwi historians also talk about the way Tiwi warriors used Gsell's flour to 'become white'. And interestingly, although everyone knows this was a disguise – a form of body paint – they note that the Tiwi made themselves into the image of white people. Another storyteller describes how the men used it:

> [Gsell] went in and he got out a tin of flour, niki niki (they call that tobacco), niki niki, mirror and he showed them. And a tomahawk. Then he got the flour and he put it on him [points

to face] ... Then they got the flour those old men. Those old men too. What I heard from the old people they told me. This story came from the old people, so we carry that on through the next generation. Well then they put the flour on themself too, to make themself white, maybe like you [Laura Rademaker]! And they felt his skin, you know. Then they felt themself. 'Oh, it's different' they must have thought, 'it's different'. And he showed them that white flour, that flour. And they got some of them and they put it on themself and they made themself white, same colour as him![43]

Tiwi used the new goods to mess up the missionaries' expectations, along with their ideas about culture and race. The objects did not mean the same thing to Tiwi as they did to the colonisers, as was true of many Indigenous peoples who received goods from Europeans.[44] In Tiwi culture, there are two occasions where you might paint yourself white: after the death of a close relative or after committing a murder.[45] The whiteness disguises the person from the deceased's angered spirit. There are Tiwi stories about murderers being found out by their whiteness. The priest's whiteness would have been the first thing Martina noticed, so 'she probably was afraid'. But 'she didn't tell him that she was afraid of him with the colour'.[46] In these stories, whiteness has sinister overtones – Gsell's whiteness is repeatedly cited as a reason for Martina to be afraid. Perhaps this is why Martina is remembered as the 'brave, brave woman'. Gsell's whiteness associated him with death, making him appear powerful and dangerous.

Rations of flour and tobacco became the means by which Tiwi eventually became more dependent on missionaries, which enabled the colonisers to govern them. Their apparent enchantment with the white goods reflects current Tiwi concerns about the allure of new technologies – Old People today talk about the internet, televisions, as well as alcohol, drugs, and cigarettes, and the impact these have on their culture and their youth. Tiwi women explain that their people have 'chained' themselves to these things and cannot live without them. Flour, perhaps, represented the death of an old way of life.

But flour was also intrinsic to the mission's ritual and material life; so important that Tiwi people came to associate the whole mission enterprise with it. The flour ration was the basis of the mission economy, to the point where another Aboriginal mission run by the same order of priest – the Little Flower Mission – gained the nickname the 'Little Flour Mission'.[47] On Bathurst Island Mission, the dormitory girls baked bread for the priests daily. They would steal dough, because they themselves had porridge and were hungry.[48] Flour was prized and in demand. Flour was also central to the missionaries' most sacred ceremony, the Eucharist, and older women remember first learning to 'receive our Lord: bread'.[49] God is present through the flour, so it became associated with missionaries' wealth and power, both spiritual and material.

But Tiwi historians themselves interpret the meaning of the flour differently. It was 'to make themself white, maybe like you [Laura]! … they made themself white, same colour as him!'[50] It made the men look like white people; this was a form of 'cultural cross-dressing'. The theme of disguising oneself, appearing like a white person, was also prominent when a younger man emphasised the 'flash' new goods in his oral history. As Romolo Kantilla explained:

> Next day, [Merapanui] tried all the goods, all the clothing. He was walking around the campsite looking flash. And the other old people was playing card. They didn't recognise him. So they call him over. He walked up looking flash. They asked him, 'hey, where did you get all the goods?'[51]

Merapanui was unrecognisable. For Tiwi people, Merapanui and Martina both played with whiteness to cross cultures and racial lines – Martina by 'marrying' the white man and living at the mission, Merapanui by using the white man's goods.

Flour rationing was meant to help assimilate First Nations people into white society, drawing them into the culture of the colonisers. But it did not. It created an ongoing relationship between black and white, but it did not create a shared culture, let alone absorb First Nations people into white culture. Rationing allowed Aboriginal people to keep their autonomy while regularly engaging with the colonisers on their own terms.[52] In Gsell's case, the Tiwi put the very substance he expected would help him subordinate them to their own, novel use. Tiwi people seem to have signalled to each other their new relationship with Europeans and the power it brought. At the same time, they showed that they would maintain their own culture, whether or not Europeans perceived what they were doing.

'Lucky Martina made the changes'

Martina herself had broader ambitions; by engaging with missionaries and living as a mission girl, she enabled a major reform of the Tiwi marriage system, loosening the requirements for Tiwi marriage partners within Tiwi kinship law.

In the Tiwi marriage system, partners were determined by both one's father's and mother's spiritual identity. They must share the same tungarima (Country group); that is, be affiliated to the same place on the islands, an identity inherited through their fathers. In Tiwi traditions, patrilineal territorial groups have long been flexible; they shift depending on competition and status of 'big men'.[53] A suitable partner must also have an appropriate totem (or 'Dreaming'), inherited through the mother. Certain totems may only marry certain others.

But Tiwi tradition tells that Martina's marriage changed things. Although Martina was from a part of the islands called Malau, the man she eventually married after she left the dormitory was from Ranku. He had the correct matrilineal totem for her but, notably, she married outside her traditional Country group, which came from her father. Martina did not envisage a European marriage system for her people. Still, by marrying outside her Country, she suggested that although Tiwi should not marry 'anyone' like whites (totem very much mattered), they could perhaps marry 'anywhere'. By loosening the nexus between marriage and place, Martina's marriage enabled Tiwi to settle and centralise on sites such as the mission.[54] Not only was she the first to settle at the mission, her marriage enabled other Tiwi to do so in large numbers. She also undercut the role of 'big men' in Tiwi society while preserving the value of matrilineal totems, which could be why she is remembered so proudly by the older generation of women today. Marriage became less about men and more about women and mothers, thanks to Martina.

According to Tiwi historians, Martina not only helped establish the community, she also pioneered new, more flexible, forms of the Tiwi promise system, suited to the mission era:

> Lucky Martina made the changes, make choices for everyone …
> Promise still given out today. We wouldn't have a choice, have a
> choice today. Everyone have a choice today.[55]

Martina gave women more freedom to reject their promised husband, another feature of modern Tiwi life. Today, the promise system still provides a structure for organising marriage, but potential partners can always say no. A number of women who went through the dormitory as girls married their promised husband today. Promises are still important to Tiwi people and regulate gift-giving and obligations, even if it is more common for women to marry their 'boyfriends' nowadays.

According to Tiwi histories, by pioneering these two major Tiwi marriage reforms, Martina used the mission to women's benefit. Brokering gifts from the white man made marriage reform politically palatable for older relatives, and demonstrating the benefits of a period of dormitory living made new forms of marriage attractive to younger women. But this did not mean the Tiwi capitulated to

Bishop Gsell's 'wives' index card 1.
MSC Archives Kensington

a western idea of how marriage and family should look. The Tiwi kinship system remained intact, and the Tiwi tradition of promises lived on.

The Tiwi accounts pose big challenges to Gsell's version. Not a single Tiwi person suggests that Martina became Gsell's wife, that they were sexually involved, or that there was any confusion around this. If Tiwi people use the language of buying and selling, it is not an important part of the story. Gsell's goods are presented as a peace offering rather than the cost of 'purchasing' a woman as Gsell made it out to be. Yes, Martina did not want to be a youngest wife, but Tiwi already had existing traditions which gave her other options, and she took them. When she ran to the priest, what was different was not that she ran, but that she ran to a white man and encountered his new goods and new Spirit.

What Gsell didn't know

Tiwi histories show that Gsell misjudged the changes to Tiwi marriage that took place beginning with Martina, as it changed according to Tiwi rather than European preferences. Martina herself might have encouraged Gsell to believe she was 'enslaved' to her husband, in need of 'rescue'. Maybe she so successfully played the part of the Aboriginal girl-victim (just what he expected to find) and 'went white' by entering the mission world, that white people didn't notice or record her work reforming Tiwi marriage. Tiwi histories depict Martina's cultural crossing as more than a way to benefit from the missionaries and mitigate their impact; it was also a kind of cultural play, like a Topsy doll playing two roles, to speak to her own people.

Part of Martina's success was that Gsell never realised (or perhaps never acknowledged) what Martina was doing; that is, how her actions worked for her own people. Martina's story, as told by Tiwi women, reveals how Aboriginal women could use unexpected circumstances to achieve changes in their own social world. They too could turn their worlds upside down for the sake of their own people. Martina's actions were not about the missionaries at all; in reforming Tiwi marriage she enabled Tiwi people to settle at the mission, in effect establishing the town that exists today.

The Tiwi are confident that Martina acted for her community. She has become a symbol of the Tiwi ability to navigate change and especially of Tiwi women's authority in community and church affairs.

The other woman, the other approach

Gsell himself admitted that not everything went smoothly in his supposed scheme of trafficking girls. Some objected. Gsell reported a Tiwi man, Sam, tried to retrieve a young woman, Helen, from the mission. Helen apparently wanted to marry Sam's brother. But according to Gsell, Sam's brother said he would 'kill her' and 'kill everyone else in the Mission' if Helen were not handed over.[56] Only having Gsell's reports to go on, it is hard to know how Helen viewed her situation.

But this was not the only incident of Tiwi people threatening to wipe the missionaries out. There is another story from that same year as Martina's great escape, hidden in the archives, that tells us about another woman who wanted change. Another woman, Fanny Garr, attempted to force the missionaries off the islands in 1916, just as the Tiwi's Ancestors had sent the British and the Portuguese away many years before.

Fanny is hard to identify. Tiwi today do not remember much about her. Her husband, Matthew Garr, was born on Thursday Island and described by visiting doctor Henry Fry as 'Malay' with a 'smattering of Tiwi'.[57] So she may have been from Thursday Island too. We don't know. Regardless of how she got there, in 1916, Fanny was living on the Tiwi Islands. Matthew went over to work at Oenpelli in 1914, and then volunteered to fight with the Australian Imperial Force in the Great War on 6 October 1915.[58] His documents note his marriage to Fanny and his address as 'Bathurst Island Mission'. Should he be killed, his personal estate would be bequeathed to Fanny. But his records also include a form with instructions about his pay; Father Gsell of Bathurst Island Mission Station was to receive four shillings per day according to an undated form signed by Matthew of the 41st Battalion of the AIF.[59] The mission 'managed' income (that is, they took it) which would normally be received by soldiers' wives. She was not receiving her due, but Fanny had a plan.

The Aborigines Protector, James Beckett, visited the islands on 11 May 1916. He found the missionaries agitated. The nuns, especially, were 'quite unnerved' and wanted to evacuate. Beckett and Father Henschke slept in the school house near the convent as bodyguards.[60] The missionaries had recently discovered a plot to kill them all.

According to Beckett, since Matthew left, Fanny had been 'very restless and impatient of restraint'. She wanted to leave the island and have access to her husband's income. Gsell said no. Then, a Tiwi man had reported to the missionaries that:

> he had overheard the men in the camp say they intended to kill all the Missionaries and take away all the Girls into the bush. The Rev. Sisters and the Father were to be killed at a certain time and the colored men on the lugger were to be killed on the return of the boat from Darwin.[61]

The missionaries quizzed others and several girls, too, admitted that they were aware of the plan and 'expected the massacre to take place on the following Sunday'.[62] Beckett identified a young man who had been living with Fanny – Louis Munkara – as the 'ring leader' of the trouble so 'locked him up'. Louis Munkara is famous to the Tiwi. As we shall see, he was central to the Tiwi's defence of their islands during the Second World War. He was also involved in the islands' defence here, in a quite different way.

According to Louis, Fanny had 'persuaded him to sleep with her in her cottage' and then 'induced him to urge the tribe to murder the missionaries and take away the Mission girls to the bush'.[63] Anthropologist Charles Hart described Louis as a 'constant seducer' as well as 'formidable fighting man … dangerous in battle'. He was also a Tikalaru man with Country near the mission. So Fanny's choice of Louis for this operation made sense on a number of levels.[64] Louis talked to the older men and they considered the plan, but insisted on waiting at least a week. During the week, Fanny was deported to Darwin. The plot fell through.

Beckett went to talk with the old men. They told him 'they did not want to harm the Missionaries who had been good to them and could not understand why any of the Mission girls had urged them to do so'.[65] Perhaps they were just telling him what he wanted to hear. Or perhaps it really was the young girls who felt particularly aggrieved by the missionaries. The old men, meanwhile, were benefiting most from the missionaries' material goods. It is not clear what changed young Louis's mind. But somehow he concluded they were better off allowing the missionaries to stay. Fanny became a war widow in 1917. Matthew was killed in action in Belgium. His war medal and victory medal were posted to her at Bathurst Island Mission in 1922.[66]

So as much as Martina was able to broker new opportunities for Tiwi women, the Tiwi community was not unified on the mission question. Some, including young women, clearly, wanted them gone. Others, like Martina, saw their future in the mission. Perhaps Fanny's failure convinced them that working with the mission was the only viable option. Louis, meanwhile, went on to become a key leader in the mission. In 1919, when a cyclone hit Bathurst Island, the missionaries reported that Louis was their man in a crisis. The cyclone threatened to rip the roof off the school; Louis ran out to tie it down, reporting later to the priests that he had saved it. He relayed urgent messages, reporting on the safety of the children.[67] By 1927, he was teaching in the boys' school; he was clearly a trusted leader.[68] As we know, Martina's approach of forming strategic alliances with the missionaries eventually prevailed, as it did for Louis. But the question of whether it was worth allowing the mission to stay, or whether the Tiwi were better off finding other allies, persisted into the war years. What might the Japanese presence mean for the Tiwi and their mission?

9

PURRAPUTUMALI, NGINYA AMINI (LOUIE, MY GRANDFATHER)

Mavis Kerinaiua

This story is about unsung Tiwi heroes who served and protected Tiwi Islands and the northern parts of Australia in the Second World War. It is in remembrance for their dedication and service to Australian war history.

I wrote this story to convey my thoughts and feeling about my aminayi (grandfather) Louie and the other Tiwi who contributed towards the island coastal watch in 1942. The Old People and my mother told us stories. The stories I heard growing up always made us proud of who we are as one Tiwi family.

Ngingani ngawa kukunari ngini warntarrana ngirramini ngawa-ampi purrukumwarri, awuta kwapi pupamurrumi kangi awarranaki World War II.

(Today we are happy because of the great achievements our grandfathers left us, those who served in the Second World War.)

Louie, my grandfather (Purraputumali), and his brother-in-law Mijaji (Matthias Ulungura) Ampurrupulayuwa my yangimani (other grandpa) first captured the Japanese pilot at Tuyu on Melville Island while caring for and protecting the women and children. Especially the toddler named Clarence who the pilot held and played with, while Mijaji came and crept behind him with a tomahawk handle used as a pistol hidden in his shirt. He said, 'stick 'em up! I am

Louis Munkara, photographed by John Brown, no date.
Justin O'Brien Collection

Hopalong Cassidy', and said it perfectly. That's what my mum told me. In those days you would watch your favourite western movie star with family, enjoying the outdoor cinema under the stars back home at the mission where the old town hall building once stood, where the childcare centre is now.

Nginya yintingala kapi ngawa amini yati Louie Purraputumali Munkara.

(I am the second youngest granddaughter of Louie Purraputumali Munkara.)

My grandfather Louie Purraputumali was a man of honour and integrity, and a strong Tiwi family man. We do not know his date of birth, but he died of tuberculosis in 1964. He was of the Yarinapinila (red ochre) clan. His mother was Pangutatuwu Elizabeth Portaminni from Wurankuwu and his father was Turimpi Pupuramapuwirri Munkara from Jikilaruwu. His first wife was Marie Assumpta Kilimatuwanga Tiparui, she was mother to Harold, Thecla, Odella and Beatrice. His second wife was Mabel Wulungura who had Harry Kwalinga and Ruth Pongkiliyanuwu, my mother. He took as his tribal duty and marital obligations to his third wife maningawu [grandmother] Consolata Munkara who was a Tarnikinga (flying fox clan). Maningawu died in the '80s at Jikilaruwu beach and was buried in a bark coffin there. I remember they all put together an SOS sign made on the beach from wood to get the coast watch plane to send help for her.

My mother told me aminayi had three canoes; one of them now lays buried in the sand at Jalayuwa beach at Jikilaruwu. He was also known to have bravely paddled one of his canoes, which he named Aku, to Jiliyarti (now Darwin) and mingled with the mainlanders and Chinese and worked at the Port of Darwin with some Tiwi men and a couple of his brothers, with their father Turimpi. Turimpi later died in Darwin when thought he saw Yaparraparri, a min-min light, and chased it with his axe and died there.[1] But it was not a min-min light, it was only the headlights of the first automobile, the Talbot car, which arrived in Darwin in the early 1900s for a world tour.

Louie was the helper at times of need. In 1919 the mission experienced their first tropical cyclone that badly hit the mission and Louie helped putting together a plan to care for the children and tying down the building in the midst of the cyclone. Later he helped rebuild after the first devastation. He was also a teacher for the boys.

You can say Louie and the mission had mutual respect and worked side by side looking after Tiwi, murrakupuni and tangarrima (people, country, and the mission). One day they were out bush working when Father McGrath got sick and my aminayi cared for him and made him warm tea to settle his stomach.

During that fateful day, 19 February 1942, Louie was in his canoe on a surveillance watch with his Munkara nephews. He later managed to capture five Japanese fighter pilots, who crash-landed their Mitsubishi plane near Melville Island.

The church roof was hit by the machine guns while everyone was out in the mangroves for safety. Louie built shelters and hunted food for the families. The Japanese plane was the first to bomb Darwin before it got hit and crashed at Melville Island.

The five Japanese who abandoned their Mitsubishi plane managed to parachute out of the plane and for 15 days floated in the water. The pilots disguised as themselves as 'Coolies' (Asian workers) from an allied ship, but Louie was quick smart and saw their badges hidden in their jackets. Louie captured them by using his spear. With the help of the young Munkara nephews he managed to get them on land and they kept a close watch on the captives while he paddled his canoe to Nguiu Mission to get help.

His nephews took watch while he went to Father McGrath to ask for a .303 rifle. But the mission ran out of ammo and only had one bullet. Father McGrath could only give Louie one bullet. Louie said he would literally line them up in one line and shoot them with just one bullet!

And he did line them up in a straight line and that is how he was given the name 'Line-em-up Louie'. They swam back to Nguiu Mission and later Father McGrath sent them to Darwin and the POWs went to the Cowra prison at NSW for two years (when they tried to escape the compound was bombed and there were no survivors).

He also swam to rescue men off the burning *St Francis* lugger at the Pumakirri Aspley Strait. He brought them to the mission and took care of them, clothed and fed them. I researched at the National Archives that my aminayi was so tired that day and lay on the beach to rest his exhausted mind and body. I can imagine how he must have felt multitasking, so everyone is safe and sound.

There were a lot of Tiwi who contributed towards the Black Watch during the Second World War. Bathurst and Melville Islander men were part of the war effort.[2] Because of their dedication and service to the war efforts we acknowledge how far they came to protect our sovereignty, the land and Tiwi culture. They were known as the Black diggers. I also heard he was in a submarine one time there and that many other Tiwi men were aboard the submarine and even went to China from Darwin.

Louie's brother-in-law is Matthias Ulungura, who captured the first Japanese pilot on Australian soil at Tuyu Melville Island. Matthias and Mabel share the same grandfather from the Wulungura side which makes relationships between the two as brother-in-law: a stronger Tiwi connection. All the unsung heroes are related in many ways and are the Tiwi warriors we follow.

My grandfather was given the title of a flight sergeant and marched in the Darwin RAAF parade wearing the uniform that was given to him for his service and dedication in protecting the Tiwi Islands. They were all given rations as payments. Later in the '60s some Tiwi men were recognised and were paid shillings. They later received compensation payments, and some awarded with medals but some never got the recognition they deserved for serving as volunteers and working just as hard for their fellowmen and country Australia.

Louie was also known as a political man, a mediator, a peace-maker, a larrikin, bit of a shenanigan, and a seducer of women and called many other names but he will always be known as 'Line-em-up Louie' and Sergeant Louie, who captured the five Japanese fighter pilots whose plane first bombed Darwin.

My aminayi is my champion my kwapini (hero) my unsung hero nginya amini Purraputumali.

Pongki (peace) I give you all mana nimpangi (goodbye).

Magdalen Kelantumama

Mavis Kerinaiua researching at the National Archives of Australia, photograph by Laura Rademaker, 2022

Pukumani memorial poles, Melville Island 1948,
Axel Poignant, National Library of Australia

Romolo Kantilla, Tiwi historian,
photograph by Laura Rademaker, 2022

Calista Kantilla, Tiwi historian and elder,
photograph by Laura Rademaker, 2016

Bathurst Island Mission, photograph by James Campbell, 1912, Library and Archives NT

Women working in a mission garden, MSC Archives Kensington

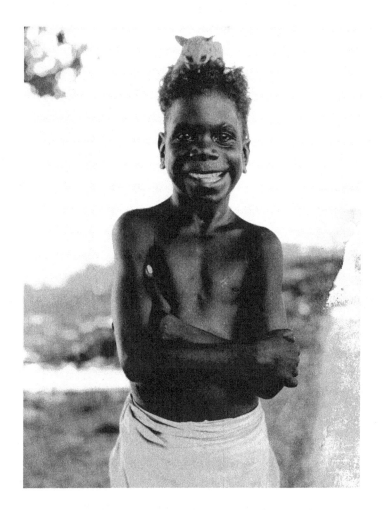

Desmond Munkara with a pet possum

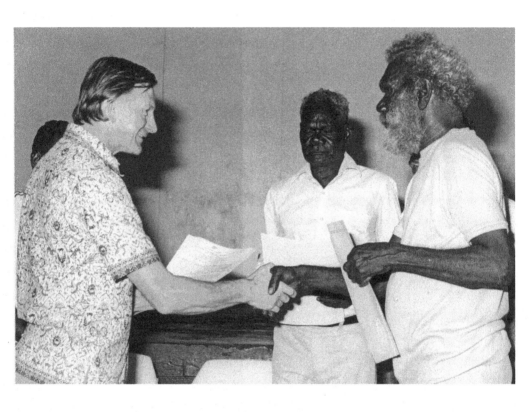

Ceremonial handover of land title deed to Bathurst Island Council
(represented by Aloysius Puntulura and Benjamin Tipiloura)
by Ian Viner, Minister for Aboriginal Affairs, 1978,
Libraries and Archives NT

10
UNLIKELY ALLIES

Laura Rademaker & Mavis Kerinaiua

Japanese they came up here. [The missionaries] kicked them out.
Didn't like them, kicked them out.[1]

Tiwi people heard the planes before they saw them. On 19 February
1942, 27 Japanese planes flew overhead on their mission to bomb
Darwin. Nine of the planes broke formation to gun the mission.[2]
Tiwi people fled, hiding in the mangroves. Louis Munkara swept up
the Tiwi kids and made a makeshift shelter in the mangroves, keeping
them safe and hidden. The women ran with their children, frightened
and also hiding in the mangroves.[3] Magdalen Kelantumama told us:

> The war was here first and they ran past here. They saw that
> plane, all Japanese plane, they were hiding themselves.[4]

Hiding in the mangroves was the smart, strategic thing to do. Just as
they had a century ago, Tiwi people used the terrain – and mangroves
specifically – to their tactical advantage. As James Darren Puantulura
explained, by doing so, they drew on long cultural tradition about
how best to use the landscape. The Japanese had guns, but Tiwi had
knowledge of Country:

> [Tiwi people] used to fight with weapon, their sticks and …
> fighting sticks, made of bamboo and a piece of log, pine, and

make it into a fighting stick. They wouldn't have machine guns like that. And that is why they ran when the war came. They were surprised, and that's why my grandmother ran … Everybody ran …

Everyone evacuated, hide in the bush, and that's why the war went to the mangrove. It's the mangrove itself, a good place to hide, because those Japanese can't get the mob because there's a lot of obstacles they can't climb, and plus they would get sinked by the mud. And that's why … the Tiwi mob had a good trick to take them in there, and that's why one Japanese, one tried to come, but apparently when he saw my grandmother and dad [Mina and Clarence], my grandmother ran inside the mangrove.

And so you can make your enemy weaker … you can direct them into the mangrove, because they have heavy boots, they will have no way of walking towards the mangrove, because there's a lot of obstacles, and a lot of predators, there's no way. So Tiwi people had brains of going in there and taking them, that's what happened.[5]

Thanks to the quick evacuation to the mangroves, only one Tiwi man, Fernando Urungarpotemeri, was injured in the raid.[6]

But some Tiwi historians also suggest that the Japanese did not shoot to kill. They tell how the Japanese planes swooped and turned, to the delight of children. One flew so close to the beach that the pilot and the children could see each other's faces. They waved and smiled. Tiwi remember that the Japanese are kin for them, thanks to the history of pearling in Tiwi waters. This meant they were family, and many Tiwi wonder if the Japanese also remembered this when they flew overhead. This was not their fight. One woman remembered how she thought the Japanese might have lollies for them:

I was about five or six, out in the bush [when the war began].
Kuwa [yes], but you know people used to come by canoe. They
used to tell people to move, move along, move along the other
side to Melville Island. Where we can [be] safe because Japanese
came from that way. Bomb in Darwin. I seen that plane and
run in the bush, hide when we saw that plane. But when we saw
a big plane and we watching that, might be that [they] throw
something, lollies for us.[7]

In white Australia's familiar histories of the Pacific War, as Tiwi
elder Magdalen Kelantumama explains, there is 'nothing said about
this community and what happened'.[8] But Tiwi historians explain
that it's impossible to understand Australia's experience of the Pacific
War on this continent without the Tiwi story. Not only were the
Tiwi the first to face Japanese bullets, but the origins of the conflict
go back to earlier disputes on their islands. This is a history of the
Second World War that most Australians have never known.

For generations, the Tiwi people had fought intruders to their
islands. But by the 1930s and 1940s, missionaries believed they had
taken over this gatekeeping role, controlling (or at least attempting to
control) who came and went. Then came the Japanese. Not that the
Tiwi themselves had problems with the Japanese. For many Tiwi, the
Japanese were friends and kin. Many liked them, even loved them.
The Japanese would become the Tiwi's trading partners and patrons,
some hoped.

But the missionaries would not share the Tiwi, and the Tiwi had
to choose. In the 1930s and 1940s, the missionaries who lived on the
islands at the Tiwi's pleasure attempted to take control, both of the
land and the Tiwi themselves. By doing this, as Tiwi explain, they
provoked the Japanese to violence.

It is not only Tiwi accounts that link the mission to armed
conflict with the Japanese. Father Gsell's fury, along with others'
outcries against the Japanese, led to an Australian patrol boat

machine-gunning a Japanese lugger in 1937. The contest for the Tiwi was central to ratcheting up white Australia's fear of a supposedly unprotected north, vulnerable to all kinds of transgressions. Tiwi relations with the Japanese exposed the missions' (and with it, white Australia's) power as limited. Priests could not control Tiwi contact with outsiders, nor could they control Tiwi actions or relationships. Tiwi people, as always, had diverse ideas and actions and feelings that could not be constrained. In the end, they fought their own fight.

A Japanese alternative

When it comes to the history of the pearling industry, Tiwi people do not tell many stories today about the relationships between Tiwi women and Japanese pearlers. On this topic, the Old People, 'they never tell us anything ... They never tell that story or anything', one woman explained to us.[9] Some still feel shame. So, we begin this story of the Tiwi and the Japanese with Gsell's account, reading Tiwi perspectives between the lines.

Two hundred Tiwi had now been baptised; half of these had been since 1925.[10] Tiwi family life, Gsell believed, had fundamentally changed. But this apparent success, he predicted, would see a backlash:

> Until now the natives have only encountered religion in theory, without really realising the consequences it could have on their lives and customs. Now that they can see religion in practice in our Christian families, they have started realising that it is no more, no less than the decline and the end of their old superstitions, and naturally many of them are reacting and fighting back. There is no doubt that for the mission this is the beginning of a difficult period, but by the grace of God, it shall triumph.[11]

But Gsell did not predict that some of the backlash would come from the dormitory girls, now grown women, themselves.

This was the heyday of the pearl-shelling industry, a dangerous business, built on Japanese and South East Asian labour, that thrived from the 1870s to 1960s in North Australia. Pearl shell (mother-of-pearl) was used to make buttons. Australia became the world's greatest source of mother-of-pearl.[12] With the White Australia Policy, foreign-owned luggers were not allowed in Australian waters. But Australian-owned luggers could still use Asian labour, provided the workers were indentured labourers and required to return to their homelands. With a 10 per cent annual death rate, few white workers were willing to do it. Indentured Asian labour was cheaper anyway. So Australian boats, crewed and captained mostly by Japanese people, scaled the coast of North Australia in search of pearl shell, including the coast of the Tiwi Islands.

The Aboriginal people who met the Japanese, in many cases, found them more trustworthy and down-to-earth than most white people. The Japanese were willing to eat and camp with Aboriginal people. They kept their word. They made no claim over Aboriginal land.[13] According to buffalo shooter and footballer Reuben Cooper in 1938, Aboriginal people looked forward to the annual pearling season, 'as it means plenty of tobacco, food and gifts'.[14]

Of course, relationships between Aboriginal and Japanese people were not always friendly. Still, as one old man from Groote Eylandt remembered, his fathers used to work with the Japanese and were paid in rice:

> They used to be working and [diving] and working with the
> aborigine people … and they pay for rice or whatever they got.
> Good people, Japanese. [15]

The pearling luggers came to the Tiwi Islands at Garden Point on Melville Island every year. The crew would replenish their water supplies and camp on the shore. Although Bathurst Island was an

Aboriginal Reserve, meaning that only missionaries and officials could visit, Melville Island was not. The pearlers were not acting illegally when they landed.[16] Gsell and his missionaries were very concerned about the pearl-shell industry. It was clearly exploitative of Asian labour, but the missionaries' concern was that it impinged on the integrity and isolation of the Tiwi mission. Here were fleets of Asian men, far from their wives and families, with ample supplies of rice and other goods. When the mission was the sole provider of flour and tobacco to the Tiwi, it thrived. Now there were other well-resourced men with a potential interest in Tiwi women.

Gsell raised the alarm to government officials in 1928. The mission, he wrote, was 'helpless against this scourge'. Old men, he claimed, were selling women to the sailors. 'Something should be done by the Government to protect the natives against their own greed and the lust of these foreign crews'.[17]

He raised his concerns again in 1931. He acknowledged the crews employed Tiwi and actually 'treat[ed] them well and [paid] them well'; however, he had three objections: the problem of 'children being enticed away' from school; Tiwi men ('boys') being given alcohol; and finally, 'immorality and prostitution'. By this stage, five children Gsell referred to as 'half caste' – children with Tiwi mothers and Asian fathers – had been born.[18]

The government did nothing, so Gsell played the media, turning to white Australia's fears of Asians. When Gsell had first described his approach of 'buying' children for his dormitory to the Catholic public, there was no talk of 'rescuing' girls. In 1918, for instance, he wrote about 'purchasing' children (not only girls) as a way 'to keep them on the station' and prevent parents from 'interfer[ing] too much'.[19] The convent consolidated the priest's influence over the children and attracted their parents to camp close by and work for the mission. Children were like a magnet.

But in the 1920s, he began to write of 'saving' girls. The dormitory was now more than a strategy to attract Tiwi families; he portrayed his 'purchases' as a moral obligation to defend Tiwi girls. In a 1929 article declaring Tiwi girls were 'Slaves to Cruel Custom', Gsell reported that 'love is unknown, greed and selfishness are at the bottom of all their matrimonial business', before explaining his mission's system of 'buying' girls. The article quoted Gsell's description of a typical Tiwi wife 'more like a degraded soulless creature than a human being'. Her Tiwi husband was supposedly her 'lord and master'; the task of the mission was 'to set young girls free' and to 'deliver' them from 'the horrible native matrimonial system'. He went on to explain the 'purchase' of Martina, claiming to have 'bought' 65 girls. According to travel writer Ernestine Hill in 1934, Gsell bought 'unwanted babies for a few sticks of tobacco, sometimes saving them from death'.[20] The *Catholic Press* also repeated the claim that Gsell bought 'unwanted children'.[21] It is not clear why Gsell would need to buy them if they were unwanted (surely unwanted children would cost nothing).

None of this matches what Tiwi historians remember and know. They tell stories of Tiwi people entrusting girls to the nuns for education and childcare. Naturally, they expected gifts from missionaries for allowing this arrangement.

Meanwhile, Gsell's rationale for 'purchasing' girls evolved again in the early 1930s. He started saying he was 'saving' girls from slavery, not only to their Tiwi husbands, but to Japanese pearlers. The two were connected in his mind, as Tiwi and Japanese men supposedly colluded in a trade of women. His 'purchase' of Martina was, he claimed, 'the beginning of my plan for rescuing children from tribesmen and from Japanese'.[22] When visiting Darwin in 1934, Gsell claimed that he had now 'purchased' 124 girls to 'save' them from Japanese pearlers.[23] He was their only hope, he wrote:

Japanese, Malays, Keepang [Kupang; that is, Indonesian] natives and other Asiatics camp at the island ... The tribal chiefs, with complete power over their followers, hand their girls over to the Japanese in return for food ... and the usual trinkets ... Compared with the scores of girls sold to the Japanese only a few have been saved by the mission. But I believe that in my method lies the only hope for the girls of the Bathurst Island tribes.[24]

The irony in Gsell depicting the Tiwi women as slaves to Asian men hides the reality that the men aboard the pearling luggers were indentured labourers themselves: effectively enslaved people. Their work was dangerous – many died from 'the bends' or drowned. In their vocal concern for the supposed 'slavery' of Aboriginal women, Gsell (and the Australian public) ignored the unfree labour of Asian men.

Gsell began to describe Tiwi girls as his own 'wives' around the same time that he started to talk of saving girls from slavery. In the early 1930s, Gsell spoke publicly to the Australian media about his system of buying girls. The story was so sensational it travelled around the world: 'Missionary Buys 124 Girls to Save Them from Slavery', read the San Francisco *Sunday Examiner* in 1934.[25] In its story, it claimed that the Tiwi misunderstood Gsell, thinking he was purchasing the girls as wives:

> Father Gsell had the usual white man's aversion to the purchase
> of a slave, but here, he felt, was a case where circumstances
> did alter cases. The priest bought the girl. The natives assumed
> that he had purchased her for a wife, and were ready to hold a
> celebration of the marriage, until the priest stopped them. He
> had bought the girl, he explained, but not with any intention of
> wedding her.[26]

There is no suggestion from any Tiwi historians, nor the early documentary sources, that Martina or any of the other girls believed they were somehow married to the priest. Gsell himself quickly complained to the *Northern Standard*, which had republished the article, saying its account was 'misleading'. Tiwi women were not technically slaves, they were simply promised as wives before birth. His payment of £2 to their promised husbands' families released girls from 'the shackles of tribal law' leaving girls 'free and able to choose a husband'.[27] Gsell was more concerned, it seemed, to correct allegations that he was engaged in slave trading. He did not correct claims that the Tiwi believed Martina became his wife. Instead, he too began referring to the girls as his 'wives' from the late 1930s onwards, as he did in an interview with the *Sydney Morning Herald*: 'I've been buying wives for the past 23 years … and I believe I have more than anyone else in the world today'.[28]

But if Gsell were to 'save' girls from the Japanese, he would need greater resources. From 1936, Gsell made public appeals for further government funding. Tiwi men, he claimed, were no longer selling their daughters to the mission because they could get more from the Japanese. His measly government subsidy of £200 a year could not compete with the pearlers' wealth. When he spoke with journalists about the 'trade' in girls, he pointed out the mission's financial situation in September 1936:

> To maintain the 2000 Bathurst Melville Islanders the
> Government gives £200 a year, but we spend more than £1 daily
> on flour and tobacco alone for the natives. Where is the margin
> for other work? The natives can be induced to abandon the
> barter of women only if the mission can fully supply the food
> which they are now forced to obtain from the Japanese.[29]

By 1936, the mission's finances were in the red.[30] In the past, Gsell had received everything he had asked for from Propaganda Fide.[31] But in 1936, he became concerned at what the international political situation might mean for his budget. Germany, Italy and Poland had stopped capital flowing abroad. By August, he had heard nothing about his annual funds from Propaganda Fide, the Catholic congregation for evangelism. The funds usually arrived in July.[32] In September, he spoke to the Australian press about needing more funds to save Tiwi girls and women from 'prostitution'. So who was really selling whom? For Gsell, the plight of Tiwi women, and the

Coconut Avenue, Bathurst Island Mission, 193[?].
Charles Micet Collection, Library & Archives NT

expense of 'buying' them, became a proxy to attract government funding and deeper public sympathy.

Gsell's reports gave the impression that the Tiwi were, perhaps, going hungry at the mission (as if they did not have the bounteous produce that came from the bush). When news of the so-called prostitution of Tiwi girls to pearlers hit the media, there were suggestions that perhaps the Tiwi engaged in the practice because they were starving. Yorta Yorta leader William Cooper and missionary Annie Lock, along with others, wrote to government officials insisting that they increase the provision of flour and provide meat so that Tiwi people would not be compelled to 'prostitute' women. Gsell also appealed to fears of communism. In the *Cairns Post*, Gsell apparently claimed that 'centuries of tribal communism had reduced Australian natives to a race of idlers'. Returning to the question of food, again, Gsell insisted that 'it would greatly help if the

Government would assist in feeding the natives', so that missionaries could focus on converting children to Christianity.[33]

Still, government officials concluded there was no food shortage and did not believe that increasing the mission subsidy would make much of a difference.[34] Bush food was still plentiful. Fish still swam in the Apsley Strait; native plants still bore fruit in season. It was only the narrow patch of Country around the mission where the usual abundance had been exhausted, meaning that if the Tiwi were to stay at the mission, they must depend on mission supplies.[35] But they could always find food elsewhere; they were not going hungry.

It also seems unlikely that there was direct competition for girls between the mission and the pearlers. Instead, Tiwi were content to work with both. Gsell claimed that, during this period of Japanese pearling, not a single girl was 'sold' to the mission; 'the Japanese offered more than we could offer'. But the mission's own records show girls continuing to be 'bought' until its records stop in 1936 with 133 girls 'bought' (and no sign of abating).[36] Gsell was 'buying' girls as toddlers; the women who were visiting the pearlers were a

Patrol boat *Larrakia*, photograph by CLA Abbott, 1938.
National Archives of Australia M 10 2/209

generation older, so there was no direct competition between the dormitory and the luggers. In 1936, Gsell claimed that, in the past, he had 'bought baby girls from parents to ensure their permanent attachment to the mission', but Tiwi fathers were now refusing to 'sell' their daughters.[37] Were Tiwi men really withholding baby girls from the mission in order to send them to the pearlers in fifteen or twenty years' time? This seems unlikely, especially given that girls graduated from the convent at that age anyway. More likely is that some Tiwi people were growing sceptical of the mission, preferring to use the Japanese as their conduit to the outside world and goods. Others, however, continued to see the mission as a source of goods and education and were happy to co-operate with both missionaries and Japanese at the same time.

Eventually Gsell's appeals gained some traction. The Department of the Interior implemented a Patrol Service in 1936 to guard North Australian waters and watch the pearlers. This was a single vessel with a crew of five and armed with a machine gun and rifles: the *Larrakia*.[38] Another vessel, the *Kuru*, joined the patrol in 1938.[39] In April 1937, the *Larrakia* fired on Japanese luggers: the 'Darwin Armada' according to the *Northern Standard*.[40] The crews were arrested, but later released.[41] The Federal Cabinet responded by outlawing all foreign vessels in the vicinity of Aboriginal reserves, to 'provide additional protection for Aboriginal women'.[42] Gsell was satisfied.

> *Grâce à la protection du Gouvernement, le trafic infâme des pêcheurs de perles japonais avec les indigènes a été presque complétement arrêté et ainsi notre œuvre sera facilité.*[43]

Thanks to the protection of the Government, the infamous traffic of the Japanese pearl-divers with the natives has been almost completely stopped which will make our mission easier.

By 1941, Australia and Japan were at war.

Tiwi women and the Japanese

Tiwi women's experiences with the Japanese were mixed. Some Tiwi women loved them; some were there to trade for valuable commodities such as rice or tobacco. Some were 'humbugged'. That is a euphemism: they were assaulted. For some, it is too painful to talk about. There is trauma around these issues. When we asked Elaine Tiparui if women were sold, the answer, as it was with others, was often 'I don't know':

> I don't know. I never heard that. [The Old People] never talked about it. But they only said we don't want that here when they see a lot of coloured kids. The priest saying 'we don't mix here' but the Old People didn't learn any English and didn't learn what that axe for and what that sugar made up for flour, bananas, they didn't have that before, after that they learn when someone teach them how to use the hand saw. And they had lugger boats they went to work on those boats.[44]

Although Elaine mentioned that there were tensions about the birth of 'coloured kids' (that is, children with Japanese fathers), from her testimony, it seems this was really a concern of the priests. Tiwi people were happy to work on the Japanese luggers. Another Tiwi woman said she did know about it, but suggested the birth of children from these relationships was acceptable:

> They used to take women, trading women for foods and axe and flour. You see those brown colour people? Japanese. Mainly from Macassans. They used to be here, make love with those people … It was okay, no problem. We got a lot of this one, 'half caste'. They used to give food you know.[45]

Some Tiwi men said it was quite normal to 'lend' wives out to the Japanese in return for flour, sugar or tea and this was not shameful.

Bede Tungutalum openly acknowledged his Japanese heritage, suggesting the Japanese and Tiwi trade was ultimately for the best; without it, he would never have been born:

> They say that the grandfather was Japanese. We got told that by them Old People. That he was Japanese. And how'd that happen? They reckon that the grandmother, her husband, you know how they made friends with them. He said, 'you wanna borrow my Missus? Give me flour, sugar or tea'. That's what they say. But they didn't see anything wrong in it. It was just something that got done. But if it hadn't I wouldn't be here![46]

As he insisted, it was the missionaries who had the problem with the Japanese, not the Tiwi:

> They just come and our people used to sell, even my own grandfather. Even my own grandfather sell his wife. I heard the story. There's Tiwis round that area. Used to sell their wives … He used to sell his wife. Used to sell. They used to sell only one wife, one girl. But he had another wife, he had 12 wives. He used to sell one. For food. Used to feed people, for taking wives. In those days. But the mission didn't like it. Kicked them out.[47]

But the women themselves felt more ambivalent about the arrangement:

> Maybe [the Tiwi women] didn't like [the Japanese]. Because they used to, Japanese used to pay them with food … That's what they used to give them. Flour, rice, tea.[48]

Another Tiwi woman explained to us that 'our grandmothers … had no men, so they're grabbing that Japanese or whatever'. When asked if the Japanese were good looking: 'Kuwa [yes]'.[49] Most likely, some did not consent at all, others were in love, and still others negotiated an ambiguous relationship with the Japanese, trying to gain what they could from a fraught situation.

Written sources from beyond the mission also give mixed accounts of what Tiwi women might have experienced. Anthropologist Donald Thomson reported that little girls taken onto the luggers 'return from boats half dead'.[50] But the other main white witness, Captain Haultain of the *Larrakia* patrol boat, insisted quite the opposite – that women received better treatment from Japanese men than they did anywhere else:

> Once girls have been broken in to visiting luggers it needs
> no great urge on the part of their husbands to continue the
> practice; girls whilst on luggers are liberally & kindly treated in
> comparison to their normal existence ashore.[51]

Haultain's proposed solution to the perceived problem of Aboriginal women mingling with Asian men was extreme, even for its day. He thought there was no point in resourcing missions with more tobacco and flour because Aboriginal desire for such things was 'insatiable'.[52] He suggested instead 'summary flogging' of Aboriginal men if their wives were found on boats.[53]

Among the files in the National Archives, there are requests from Aboriginal women for permission to marry Malay pearlers. In one case, a Malay man named Barabin Juda, who had worked at Thursday Island for eight years, wished to marry a pregnant Aboriginal woman. The two were allowed to marry, but government officials didn't like it; the marriage undermined the White Australia policy. Gsell probably knew of the incident, as the Catholic missionaries also had a presence on Thursday Island. He may have even known the couple.[54] In 1930, the Department of the Interior issued a warning that any indentured labourers who 'became married to or consorted with local women' would be deported.[55] Government officials claimed that indentured workers on pearling luggers formed these attachments in order to remain in Australia but also that they would leave Australia and abandon their Aboriginal wives.[56] The men who were deported were very persistent. Some were caught returning to Broome – and to their Aboriginal lovers – under false names.[57] Despite the government policy, marriages between Aboriginal women and Asian labourers continued in the 1930s.[58] Some religious leaders dissented from the government policy; for example, the Anglican Bishop of Carpentaria wanted to allow such marriages on Thursday Island.[59] And at least one of the interracial marriages between an Aboriginal woman and an Asian labourer was celebrated in the mosque in Broome.[60]

There is also evidence that Aboriginal women moved around by land to meet their lovers at each port. Gsell frequently emphasised that some of the women involved with the pearlers were married to Aboriginal men with leprosy.[61] He intended to stir up fears of disease and to associate this with racial mixing. But the fact of leprosy also suggests that the pearlers may have been more attractive to these young women than their diseased husbands. The romance was real.

When the *Larrakia* patrol boat came to inspect the pearling luggers, Tiwi women made sure that officials found it very hard to find evidence that they were aboard. Women just jumped into the water and swam away or used their canoes to return to shore. Interestingly, their escape suggests that they were more afraid of white officials than the pearlers. When the government patrol vessel neared the pearling luggers, the Tiwi women aboard made no indication of any desire to be rescued.[62] And by leaving the boats, they protected the pearlers from arrest and prosecution.

Where pearlers were arrested for having Aboriginal women aboard, Tiwi women were evasive in the courtroom, avoiding incriminating anyone. Often they simply did not respond to questions. Other times they failed to understand questions, perhaps feigning ignorance of pidgin English. It seems they gave false names too. 'Me Ruby', said one Tiwi woman, and 'Me Ruby too', replied the second. The court recorded their names as 'Ruby 1' and 'Ruby 2'.[63]

Perhaps they were both Ruby. Perhaps they didn't understand English. Perhaps they simply sought to confuse proceedings.

It is difficult to work out the identities of the women who went to the pearling luggers. There is evidence that they were associated with the mission; some reports mention that they were 'not myalls', meaning they had some engagement with the colonising culture.[64] Some of their names are given in court reports as Lena, Melba, Marie, Kitty, Jessie and Norah.[65] Marie could be Marie Therese from the dormitory records. If so, she had been 'bought' by Gsell in 1931 at age six and was now in her mid-teens. Lena had been 'bought' in 1927. Both Marie and Lena had been promised to a man with leprosy. The women were from Bathurst Island and were wearing 'bag skirts' and 'bare above the waist': the clothing of the mission.[66] This suggests that at least some of the girls involved with the pearlers were mission girls who had been through the dormitory.

The trial of one of the pearlers, Kusumoto, was published in the *Northern Standard*. The women involved were Mary, Topsy, Agnes and Paulina, 'all from Bathurst Island'. The women said almost nothing to their interrogators, protecting the pearlers. Their answers were mostly 'me no savvy', and even with an interpreter, the prosecutor found that 'little good resulted from it'. Paulina acted 'oblivious to any of the prosecutor's questions' by putting her hand over her mouth and turning her back to him. When she finally did speak, her voice was so quiet that it was difficult to understand what she said. According to the newspapers, Topsy's evidence, likewise, was 'practically useless'.[67] The case was dismissed.[68]

Kicking the bucket

When the Japanese guns hit the mission, Father McGrath ran to the radio hut to warn officials in Darwin of the approaching disaster. He was ignored. 'Brother McGrath tried to warn, rang Darwin and they didn't believe him', Tiwi historian Bernard Tipiloura remembers.[69]

Magdalen Kelantumama explained that 'the [officials] never take any notice of him' so it was a 'shock when the [Japanese] bombed Darwin' in February 1942.[70]

Today, the radio hut has a memorial plaque, a testimony to the priest's desperate pleas. But that site has other meanings for Tiwi women that have been obscured by its significance in the history of the war: it was a birthing site. As Tiwi woman Henrietta Hunter explained:

> She [mum] said, the radio hut, that's where the girls used to go to have their babies when they was pregnant. And there's not recognition of that, it's all about how the priest was there, radioing Darwin that the Japanese was going bombing. Before that, young girls was in there having babies. And I was actually quite shocked, I said, 'what?' I said, 'Mum, that's history there. For you to remember that as a young girl here, there should be a plaque there in recognition of all you young girls who was actually midwives'.[71]

With Tiwi people dispersed into the bush and the mission nuns evacuated (the Sisters did not return until 1945), the mission was barely in operation following the Japanese invasion.[72]

For the Tiwi, the bombing of North Australia began with the missionary provocation of the Japanese. Missionaries were so incensed by Japanese relationships with Tiwi women and so disturbed by the birth of children with Japanese heritage that they expelled the Japanese from North Australia, provoking a Japanese counterattack. The 'mission didn't like it, kicked them out'.[73] The story revolves around Father McGrath's refusal to provide the Japanese with water and their violent retaliation. As a Tiwi historian explained:

> That father, Fr McGrath, he saw those Macassan[74] family to fill water in one of the tap and when he saw them he didn't like it.

He didn't like it because there were a lot of coloured children running around community. He didn't like them. 'Don't come here'. And he kick all that bucket of water, kick all the water out.[75]

Elaine Tiparui reminded us that the reason the priest would not assist the thirsty Japanese was his racial prejudice. Anything to stop more children with Japanese heritage being born to Tiwi women:

They had a lugger here … Bishop Gsell or Father McGrath. There came some men and he saw that Japanese in the lugger … *Yampajukuni*, that means the shell, that's the shell. Father saw the little babies with the colour. And he counted them. I can't remember the names of people. And he said, 'water, water, water' they said. We had a well, round here. And that bucket he threw down, Father McGrath. They wanted water and Father McGrath said 'no, go away. We got a lot of this one here [points to skin indicating colour], we don't want that' … When Father McGrath saw that bucket they come and shoot that house over there. That story told by our great, great grandmothers. Then they bomb, they bomb Darwin.[76]

The priests caused great offence. So came the aeroplanes:

My parents told me the story from the World War 2. You know, McGrath how he tipped the bucket of water and how he got angry, how them, the I don't know what we call them, I don't like calling them enemies. Japanese. They flew over and all these people have a look up, 'too many aeroplanes going past'.[77]

As Walter Kerinaiua Jnr tells the story, the offended Japanese man made a promise to McGrath, foreshadowing the attack that was to come – a 'present' for the mission:

Brother McGrath ran down the hill, 'What are you doing with the bucket? Get out of here!' Then the Japanese turned around, and said, 'we'll send you a present'.[78]

Others say it was Gsell himself who started the war:

So they came pick up water, water at the well. So he kicked the bucket. That's what made the war now. Them Japanese … the Bishop he kicked that bucket of water of them. Bishop, bishop yeah bishop, because they was humbugging too much women.[79]

The Tiwi remember that the missionaries' fear that children would be born to Japanese fathers meant that they would not tolerate the Japanese presence, driving them out by refusing them water. The war that ensued then was, in part, a competition between Japanese and missionaries over the Tiwi.

The Garden Point Mission

The Tiwi were right that the missionaries were horrified by the birth of children of mixed heritage. They watched on as the Garden Point Mission (now Pirlangimpi) was established in 1941, not far from the ruins of the Fort Dundas base. The priests stole the children born of encounters with Japanese men away from their mothers for life at the Garden Point Mission. A small solace for them at least was that, compared to other members of the Stolen Generation, their Tiwi families were not too far away (although some were sent to other Catholic missions as far away as Central Australia). Pirrawayingi Marius Puruntatameri, who today lives at Pirlangimpi, explained the town's sad origins:

Because the government set up this community for the Stolen Generation. Right? So they sent missionaries here with that idea. So the nuns were – had a lot of these – I don't mean to be offensive, but 'half caste' people, that were dragged away from their families and brought here.[80]

Unlike the missionaries and government, Tiwi people themselves accepted children born to Tiwi mothers as Tiwi, no matter their heritage:

We had a lot of Chinese, Japanese kids around. Japanese here and over in WA. In Broome. Lota mix up kids. Yeah but, they still even invite kids as well. Why not? They're human beings as well you know. Yeah I liked them. I like about families. They're still Tiwi no matter what colour you are.[81]

Garden Point Mission was established exclusively for Aboriginal children of mixed heritage. Some children had European fathers, some had Japanese or Malay. Some of the children had been taken from other parts of the Northern Territory, as far away as Central Australia. Some were taken from their family on the Tiwi Islands. Once on Tiwi Country, Tiwi people kept an eye on the children. Many were adopted into Tiwi families. Today, Tiwi people have connections with First Nations people all over the continent, thanks to their care for the children taken to Garden Point.

The Garden Point Mission did not last long. When Darwin was bombed in 1942, the children were evacuated to the southern states (whereas Tiwi children that missionaries referred to as 'full blood' were left to hide in the bush with their families). But, after the war, it opened up again. The mission operated until 1969 when people who once had been forcibly sent there endured another removal, this time to Darwin.

The history of Garden Point (Pirlangimpi) is worthy of a book in itself. Given that the children there were taken from all over the Territory, and that the missionaries believed in a different future for these children, the story is a different one to that of Wurrumiyanga.

Marie Munkara, Mavis's relative, tells these stories in her books and we commend them to you.[82]

The Tiwi war effort

Given how the missionaries had behaved, were Tiwi people perhaps tempted to side with the Japanese in this conflict? The RAAF were concerned that Aboriginal people could be a possible security threat in North Australia.[83] The missionaries, it seems, suspected that the Tiwi had at least contemplated the possibility of a Japanese alliance. According to Gsell in 1942, for 'more than 20 years' the Japanese had been telling Aboriginal people that 'they will come and be their bosses one day'.[84] And perhaps they would make better 'bosses' than the missionaries. Gsell himself indicated that the Japanese gave rich material rewards, and Tiwi people still remember the generosity of the pearlers; that they supplied rice, tea and flour.

The Tiwi had tolerated, even welcomed the Japanese to their islands for decades. But in the war, they sided with the missionaries. They had many possible reasons to do so. Like the Tiwi, Yolngu people of north-east Arnhem Land also fought against the Japanese in the Northern Territory Special Reconnaissance Unit that patrolled the coast of the Northern Territory. Yolngu considered themselves allies, not subjects, of white Australia.[85] For the Yolngu, fighting against the Japanese enemy was an opportunity to unite rival Yolngu clans. It was a means of strengthening Yolngu society.[86] The Tiwi, too, across both Bathurst and Melville Islands, could use the Japanese presence to put aside old differences. The mission had been attractive for its potential to broker peace among Tiwi clans. Now, siding with missionaries against the Japanese could be another opportunity to pursue unity.

So the Tiwi joined the war effort. Along with other Aboriginal people, they built the crucial military infrastructure around the Top

Gasimar with RAAF officer.
Justin O'Brien Collection

End.[87] Some joined the North Australian Reconnaissance Unit (later absorbed into the 56 Port Craft Company).[88]

But Tiwi did not need to go far or formally enlist to contribute. The war was already on their land and sea Country. A voluntary patrol of Aboriginal men, based at Snake Bay on Melville Island, guarded the coast and especially the airstrips on the Tiwi Islands in 'the Black Watch'.[89] Their surveillance continued a long tradition of knowing Country, observing comings and goings, and defending Tiwi land: 'looking after Country'. When the *Don Isidro*, a US supply vessel crewed by Filipinos, was bombed and sank in Tiwi waters, Tiwi formed the rescue crew. Tiwi had likely never seen so much death. As historian Magdalen Kelantumama told it:

> My Mum told me the story about her father when they shot the Japanese ship, you know, bombed that ship, Don Isidro. And there were few men his brother's cousins and their children, they was all camping at Fourcroy. And then when that ship, from the Japanese bombed that ship, and few of them Philippines … they got drowned, some of them got killed from thing. My grandfather and his family, his cousin brothers, their children, they buried a lot of them down the beach at Fourcroy. Then after that, they buried them and then they came walking down. They didn't have no cars, no nothing. They had to walk down from Fourcroy, right up to here, mission. And they told them they buried some Filipinos there who were on that ship … And they were really sad, really sad. A few of them had to come back and tell Father McGrath that they've been there, you know, those people, burying them.[90]

The Tiwi are proud of their actions during the war. A couple of days after the gunning of the mission, an unarmed Tiwi man, Matthias Ulungura, captured a Japanese pilot who crashed on Melville Island. The missionaries reported on his bravery. As Matthias was 'nonchalantly ambling through the bush', unarmed, he snuck up on the Japanese soldier, 'cleverly snatching his revolver'.[91] But the missionaries did not know the whole story.

When everyone ran to the mangroves, a toddler, Clarence, was somehow left behind in the hasty evacuation. As Tiwi historian Karen Tipiloura tells it, the story is reminiscent of the ancient woman Pima, whose child was left in the shade:

My grandmother told the story … they were probably getting
honey or bush tucker while she left Clarence sleeping in the
shade. The Japanese came, and all of them started running, and
she forgotten about her son sleeping. They were running, run
from the camp, they left him when the Japanese came and pick
him up, and he was crying, and he was sad, and he was sleeping
there.[92]

A Japanese fighter pilot had crashed and was wandering the bush.
Finding the little Clarence (as told in the previous chapter by Mavis),
he picked up the child and played with him. Once they realised
what had happened, the Tiwi sent Matthias, unarmed, to rescue the
toddler. Matthias got the idea from Hopalong Cassidy. James Darren
Puantulura, Clarence's son, told the story:

Matthias came at the back and poke him with a stick, and
pretended he's got a gun, but he had a stick. And he put his
hands up, and he let go of my dad. Put the baby down.[93]

Frances Kerinaiua also told his story:

When they had war and nobody had a gun here. One of the
Japanese got lost in the bush. He was alive. He was walking
around and he didn't look. He got lost somewhere there in the
bush and he came up, he had only axe, Japanese he had a gun.
And uncle Matthias went, 'stick em up', 'stick em up'. He was
pretending and he had real gun. He said 'stick em up'. And he
got gun off him. And he turn around and he saw he had an axe.
And they walked at Paru. And he put the gun up, boom, like
that. And everyone was surprise because they had no guns or
anything like that, they was surprised because he was the first
man to fire the gun. And then he bring that Japanese here and
then Bishop took him back to Darwin.[94]

Apparently there was some confusion. Perhaps the pilot was not familiar with Hopalong Cassidy; he did not know how to 'stick 'em up'. But as Karen Tipiloura explained, Matthias was so convincing that the Japanese pilot went along with it, despite the linguistic differences:

> Matthias said something to him, 'you give me the boy'. And the Japanese didn't understand what he said in Tiwi. And Matthias didn't understand Japanese language. Yeah, it was all complicated, there was two couldn't understand each other, because he was speaking in his language, and Matthias was speaking his language. So they didn't know what to do, so he had to hand over the boy. [95]

The fighter pilot was Hajime Toyoshima, who became the first Japanese prisoner of war captured in Australia. He was sent down to the camp at Cowra, Wiradjuri Country. He gave the Australian officials a false name, due to the shame of capture, but you can visit his grave in Cowra today.[96]

Louis Munkara, one of the sons of Turimpi, was another who defended his Country. The missionaries recognised Louis's leading role. They called him the '"number one" black boy at an Air Force Radar station', and reported him parading his uniform to other Tiwi men.[97] He became an honorary flight sergeant with the RAAF. Louis led the party that captured the crew of a crashed Japanese bomber, surrounding them and demanding their weapons. This was how he gained the nickname of 'line-em-up Louis' among the Tiwi. As described in chapter 9 he offered to stand his prisoners in a line, shooting them with a single bullet (to save the mission's precious ammunition). According to Brother Pye, Tiwi people often hunted kangaroos in this way anyway, waiting until the animals aligned, taking two in a single shot.[98] Magdalen Kelantumama, his granddaughter, has the story:

And you know what my grandfather said to Father McGrath?
Give me one bullet and I'll shoot five. And it was really funny.
You should have gone to see their surprise.[99]

But she also remembered that Louis 'never mentioned' the story of his work in the war, even though he was 'really brave'. Perhaps, like so many who witnessed these horrors, he found it hard to talk about. He died of tuberculosis, his work unrecognised by governments.[100] Magdalen learned the stories from her mother.[101] As his son wrote, 'his name will never be forgotten'.[102]

Some Tiwi were involved in covert operations. Charlie One Tipakalippa and Strangler Pungautji McKenzie spoke Malay and so were chosen for reconnaissance visits to occupied Timor on allied submarines.[103] Their relatives remember this, although interestingly, believed that they were in fact working for the Japanese – perhaps they did not even reveal the nature of their work to their families. Their memories suggest there was little enmity towards the Japanese:

We hear the Old People talking about the Japanese coming
here, picking up Tiwi men to work with them, even the Japanese
came here during the Second World War. They – Anne's relative,
uncle, father's cousin, he went with submarine with the Japanese,
travelled. Travelled around and when he came back – there's a
few of them – when they came back, they even spoke Japanese.[104]

After the war, in 1963, a group of Tiwi men approached the military and Commonwealth Government claiming wages for their war service: Cyprian Ulungara, Bismark Kerinaiua, Alan Papajua and Matthias. They pointed to their service in the Black Watch, a First Nations reconnaissance unit that patrolled the Northern Territory coast.[105] The army found no record of their service but believed it was possible they were 'employed in a civilian capacity under local arrangement'.[106] Eventually, Matthias received an ex-gratia payment – his work in capturing a Japanese prisoner of war was well attested.

The others received nothing.[107] In 1973, Louis's son, Harry Munkara, applied to the Department of Aboriginal Affairs, pointing out that his father's work was never recognised.[108] Nothing was done. In 1991 the Commonwealth Government Department of Defence, finally, compensated Tiwi people for their work in the war.[109]

Rebuilding and expanding

When the conflict was over, things changed again for the Tiwi at the Bathurst Island Mission. From 1941, the mission began receiving Child Endowment payments from the Commonwealth Government; its financial situation became more secure. That year, Melville Island joined Bathurst Island in becoming an Aboriginal Reserve, giving the mission greater control over who came and went. The Garden Point Mission re-opened, forming a crucial hub for the mission on Melville Island, to complement the work at Bathurst.

Whereas before the war, the missionaries tried to cut the Tiwi off from other influences, by the end of it, Tiwi were globally connected like never before. For Tiwi people, the war expanded their horizons even further. Now they saw that they could play an important part in national, and even international, affairs. Many, through their service with the military, saw the wealth and opportunities that might come from work in Darwin and beyond. They had forged networks with their neighbours, Aboriginal people on the mainland. They also developed kinship connections with Aboriginal people all over the Territory through their adoptive relationships with the stolen children at the Garden Point Mission. Tiwi became more ambitious. Although, in the 1950s and 1960s, the mission was able to consolidate its authority on Tiwi Country, Tiwi people were already beginning to imagine what the future of self-determination could look like for them.

11

THE MISSION DAYS

Calista Kantilla

First of the first, first of January 1938, I was born. We was out bush. I didn't born here, I born out bush. Dad and Mum brought me here right here, then Mum brought me from bush, to be baptised. Because priest was here, have children out in the bush, they'd bring their children here to get baptised. They bring all the children in for baptism then go back bush. Five-year-old I was. I was in the bush. So Mum and Dad brought me there when I was six, convent. They left me.

They were pagan, my parents, but when Brother Elliott came, they used to work with Brother. They get baptised. Used to work out at Garden Point Mission day. Mum and Dad used to work at mission, Garden Point, with Brother Barrett looking after goats and pigs. They used to come and pick me up all bush holiday. Since I wasn't married, but they used to come and visit me.

The dormitory, it's good. The convent strict more, when we were naughty, when we'd be cheeky. We used to swear at them [nuns]. We didn't like the nuns telling us what to do. So we used to have smack on our hand. Stick or strap, strap, belt.

But we didn't have pen and paper now. We still have the slate with chalk. I used to go to school underneath that old church. We used to go to school there, underneath the church. Since when they built that new school. But we never used to write pen or paper, only chalk, slate.

There used to be farm there, where the grove farm. We used, from dormitory we used to go and steal some watermelon. 'Girls, what are you doing there?' 'We're looking for banana and watermelon.' Sister, she used to tell us, 'Go on get some milk from goats'. We used to put it in the bucket, and one of my other sisters went and got some pawpaw, they were ripe ones, and she was cutting it up. Magdalene she was my cousin sister. She's the one she went in the garden to get some pawpaw. She was cutting that pawpaw. That goat used to come and let us know that somebody coming. We stole that pawpaw.

Then we used to, in the dormitory, 'Come on girls, we got to go hunting'. Where to? This place used to be bushes. They used to take us out. Sundays, only Sundays. We used to go out get some mussel. And we used to bring it back and take it with convent and cook it there. Good one.

Old church, all family used to go to church every morning, every Sunday. I remember they used to come. That church used to be full. These days I think that there's not much. It used to be beautiful there, church. We still have choir, lovely choir. It's big. Well we teach some of the young women because we talk to them about the old days. They used to love singing in Latin.

I got my promise from Mum and Dad. And Mum used to come and talk to me about him. 'I don't want you to get married to other man. Only my son.' He used to bring present for me. He used to work at RAAF, Air Force a long time. They used to work the Air Force and Army. Mission days he used to work Air Force. Easter time and he used to bring me present, like skirt and top, and something like that.

We used to work here, around the mission. Help nuns like doing laundry and baking bread. I used to do laundry, baking bread, cooking our own bread, not from Darwin. But this time they stop it. They only got bread from Darwin. We used to work hard. And we didn't have proper money.

Remember when Pope came to Alice Springs and Darwin? Remember that? I was at Alice Springs when I met him. Me and my husband. But he said, 'Christian faith is same. Love our culture' because God gave us culture, Tiwi culture, and church.

12

CREATING A SANCTUARY

Laura Rademaker
& Mavis Kerinaiua

Tiwi people often say that they have two religions: Catholicism and footy (Aussie Rules, that is). The missionaries brought both to the Tiwi Islands. Tiwi footballers are among the best in the league, and the local team – the Tiwi Bombers – dominates the Northern Territory football competition. Footy pilgrims from all over the Territory traverse the Apsley Strait to watch Tiwi play on the grounds of Wurrimiyanga every year.

Catholicism does not quite draw the crowds that football does, and these days there's some disquiet among the elders over the way footy, when played on a Sunday, distracts from Mass. But whenever there is a funeral, the Catholic traditions are a source of comfort. With the Catholic school at the heart of the Wurrumiyanga community, the rites of First Communion and Confirmation are joyful times. This religion also has deep roots in the community.

For Tiwi people, coming to terms with the mission days is a complicated business. Looking to the two 'faiths' it left, the mission's legacy is entwined in some of the very best, most celebrated aspects of Tiwi life. Its traditions draw Tiwi together even today.

But there are other parts of the mission story that divide Tiwi. This is because Tiwi people experienced the mission days differently from each other; there is no one story of the mission times. Some families experienced a time of stability and learning. Others

The mission church and community, 1954.
MSC Archives Kensington

endured humiliation and violence. Some went through a confusing combination of both. This chapter, we hope, reflects the messiness of these stories.

The post-war era

The decades after the Second World War were the heyday of the mission that, by this stage, was known as 'Nguiu'. Free from interferences by buffalo shooters, pearlers and Japanese invaders, it was a time of stability. For many Tiwi people, this was a time of opportunity; they had the chance to complement their Tiwi knowledge with western techniques in agriculture, medicine and midwifery, linguistics and literacy, music and art. Many of the Tiwi men from the mission (but few Tiwi women) could travel to Darwin and beyond. But it was also a time when the mission consolidated its control over Tiwi lives. With government backing, Tiwi people had been designated 'wards of the state' and the missionaries (ostensibly) were put in charge.

After the Second World War, the Commonwealth Government changed its policy approach for Aboriginal people. Assimilation was the its goal, and they would use missions to achieve it. At the time, many white people actually celebrated assimilation as a new, supposedly enlightened and anti-racist approach, in contrast to the old segregation and 'protection' policies. The new policies assumed that Aboriginal people were not inherently racially inferior, simply culturally 'backward' (as if this were a compliment). Given educational opportunities, they would soon blend seamlessly into white Australia; something white Australia previously thought possible only for Aboriginal people with European heritage. In 1958, the minister for territories, Paul Hasluck, explained:

> The Commonwealth and State Governments agree that the only future for Australia's 74000 aborigines is assimilation and, with the cooperation of the Christian missions, are working towards that end.

> In its simplest terms assimilation means that, to survive and prosper, the aborigines must live and work and think as white Australians do ... [1]

According to this policy, Aboriginal people would eventually enjoy the rights and responsibilities of citizenship, once they had learned to live in a citizenly (that is, white Australian) way. On paper, Aboriginal people were already full Australian citizens. But just as children are citizens who must wait until adulthood to exercise their rights, so Aboriginal people were made wards of the state until some undefined future time when white Australia would judge them to be 'mature'. Really they were citizens in name only. But the Catholic missions had their own ideas about assimilation, with distinct results for Tiwi people.

Although the mission project gave the appearance of control, it showed signs of unravelling. The mission struggled to attract staff to run the community. It lacked funds to build crucial infrastructure (although, as we shall see, some of the financial shortage was self-inflicted). The priests and brothers were getting disgruntled (as were, most likely, some of the nuns). Bishop John O'Loughlin took over from Gsell in 1949. The mission staff came to see him as a micro-manager with an old-fashioned outlook. Meanwhile, Tiwi people themselves began clamouring for greater freedoms. The mission's assumption that Tiwi people needed to be 'looked after' was increasingly difficult to justify. By the late 1960s, change was inevitable.

The garden's fruit

The children used to sneak fruit from the mission garden. Sometimes they would go in at night. Other times, they would pluck a piece while they worked. It was risky. In 1934, one young Tiwi man, Marraki, paid with his life, shot dead. It was an accident, the missionaries said, but Tiwi people were not so sure. The superintendent, Father Henschke reported what happened to his superior in Sydney:

A most unfortunate thing happened at Bathurst Island. Alphonso on Wednesday night fired a gun to frighten some blacks who were stealing his mangoes. He hit one in the leg. It was dark & he could not see anyone. They brought the [n*****] to Darwin & the Dr amputated his leg, but he died. So Alphonso was arrested. It came up before the Court today & Alphonso was acquitted in misadventure. Fr Gsell, Bro Fannon had to give evidence. Alphonso cannot return to the mission or the blacks will kill him.[2]

Alphonso was one of the first lay missionaries to come to the island with Gsell, so Gsell seemed more concerned about the termination of Alphonso's service than the manslaughter (or was it murder?) of the fruit 'thief'. Gsell wrote that he'd had to send Alphonso away from the island, even though he believed that he had only accidentally killed a 'native'.[3] The Tiwi evidently believed otherwise.

Today, Tiwi people tell the story, through song, about the poor boy who was shot dead by the 'manila man'.[4] On one level, it is a song about the murder in the mango tree, but on a deeper level, it's a song about suffering and injustice. Tiwi sing it at funerals, a reminder that they still suffer injustices.

Decades after the death of Marraki, children were still 'stealing' fruit from the garden.[5] They are senior women now. 'We were hungry', they remember.[6] Constant hunger was a recurring theme in their testimonies. As they were cutting fruit for sale in the mission store, they would whisper to each other: 'ripe one'.[7] They hid the fruit in their pockets as they worked in the garden.[8] They used Tiwi language to outmanoeuvre the nuns and priests:

> In those days, [nuns] used to go strict on us. We used to get
> hungry. We used to go back up the dormitory, lot of bananas,
> watermelon, peanuts. And when we watch out for her, she can
> come round and see us, we just go and help ourself. We steal
> from the garden. And some of them when we were in the garden
> stealing it, they keep an eye out. They keep an eye out and they
> call out when she's coming, they say, 'She's coming!' you know, in
> Tiwi. In Tiwi, 'she's coming *abanwuja abanwuja*'. That's in Tiwi
> means 'she's coming'. She never understand nothing.[9]

Sometimes some of the girls would doubt themselves. Hadn't they learned the ten commandments? They reminded each other 'this is not to touch, not to steal': '"we don't steal" we say to each other, "this is not good to steal, we know that thou shalt not steal"', but then, 'every time "hey friend, ripe one ... that pawpaw is ripe, bananas are yellow'".[10] If anyone persisted in pious doubts, other girls would quickly silence them. Perhaps they were the hungriest:

> And then someone used to say, 'thou shall not steal' because they were the commandments. And we used to say, 'if you dob us in and tell the nuns we're going to get a hiding, we're going to bust you up', we say. Yeah, naughty.[11]

Punishments for the 'theft' of fruit were a 'whacking', a 'smack', a 'proper hiding' or the 'strap'.[12] The old Tiwi women said they would always confess if caught; it gave them a better chance of avoiding the belt.[13]

But whose fruit was it anyway? The Tiwi girls planted, picked, and prepared it. It grew on their Country. So who was stealing from whom? Bernard Tipiloura, on reflection, explained that the furor over forbidden fruit was really a missionary misunderstanding of Tiwi communal life: 'A priest never realise we share food in the community ... We thought that everything was, you know, plants for us to eat'.[14]

Dormitory life

If families relinquished their daughters to the dormitory (often under various forms of duress), they remained close by, to keep an eye on the girls' welfare. Often, they set up camp on the beach. Through this proximity, they were drawn into the mission economy. They could exchange their labour for rations and, later, for pay. They might begin attending Catholic ceremonies. Sometimes families would return bush, but they would never leave for too long; they needed to be able to check on their girls.

So the girls were valuable to the mission for the way they drew their families into its orbit. But they were also a source of income and labour. From 1941, the Commonwealth Government made

Child Endowment payments available to institutions that took care of children. This meant that the dormitory girls could be a source of income; the mission received compensation for every girl on its rolls. The girls also worked to supply the mission store with fruit and bread. The store was the only source of produce on Bathurst Island – except, of course, from the bountiful kitchen of the bush. So whatever money Tiwi people earned, working for the mission or the military, or in Darwin, was circulated through the store and back into the mission's accounts. The store kept the mission running.

Together with the nuns, the dormitory girls also kept the priests well-dressed and fed. Of course, the nuns were not paid for their work, and neither were the girls. Writing back to Sydney in 1943, Father Henschke was impressed. He had a 'lovely time' thanks to this female labour:

> I had a lovely time on Bathurst. The black girls are doing wonderful work, trying to keep the place going like the Sisters. They do all the cooking, backing, washing, ironing, mending, set the vestment for Mass, the altar for Benediction, look after the sanctuary, keep the presbytery clean etc. I felt they must get great blessings for their faith & goodness.[15]

The girls worked hard, but they also had fun. The senior women today remember their schooling mostly very fondly. They talk about how they had to write with chalk on slates, rote learning their letters. Even so, their school was terribly understaffed and under-resourced, although they might not have known the extent of it at the time. A damning government report from 1964 stated that, for 150 girls on the school roll, there was only one qualified teacher. None of the teachers had any experience in teaching English as a second language. They were, no doubt, under intense stress. The children, meanwhile, were robbed of the education they deserved, but did the best they could.[16] For Magdalen Kelantumama, the worst of it was that her language was forbidden.[17] This was actively harmful:

They were strict in those days, yeah … they were really strict, those nuns. Never used to speak our language, you know. Forbidden to speak Tiwi in those days. [18]

Despite this destruction, there were things to look forward to. The older women's faces light up talking about the sports carnivals and the musical eisteddfods. As Teresita Puruntatameri remembered, 'athletics, long jump, weightlifting. We had everything!'[19] Another Tiwi woman described the daily routine. Their days were packed. The girls were proud of their accomplishments, showing off their ability to their families:

In the afternoon we play sports like basketball or softball. And we had competition from the other school like Milikapiti or Garden Point. They had a big sport day for us, it's called school sport. And parents used to come and have a look at us. And then in the afternoon we used to do our chores again, like cleaning up, brush our teeth, go and have shower, clean clothes. Five o'clock comes, tea, time for tea. Then we used to go to bed. Have a little relaxation like singing. In the afternoon we used to have singing, play the guitar, piano. The nuns taught us. This is our hobby in the afternoon. So we were like training, sports and everything. We used to have our own guitar play, music, singing. The nuns taught us how to sing properly, so we became singers.[20]

The girls were encouraged to excel at sport, although football was just for the boys. Marie Cecile Tipiloura spoke fondly of how her father, Christopher 'Foxy' Tipungwuti, was given responsibility for running the 'drill' in the morning; daily athletics for the children.[21] He also helped in the school, where he taught traditional Tiwi dances.[22] On sports days, the girls would compete in the colours of the four houses, each colour bearing the name of a Catholic saint:

We used to have a lotta sport in mission days. We have four colours. Red, yellow, blue, green. Mine was Saint Martin. I'm red. Each colour had a saint. Saint Patrick had the green.[23]

We line up, you know, marching along, with dress. Red, amber and green. That's the only. We had tie that colours of the team, sport. We had sports every afternoon. Outside the airstrip. Long time.[24]

Other girls were more musically inclined. Every year, a group would go to Darwin for the eistedfod. 'We used to sing on the stage and we used to win trophy, and everyone came along and have a look at us singing.'[25]

On the weekends and during school holidays, girls were released from the dormitory to stay with their families. They were never entirely cut off from Tiwi social or cultural life as happened at other missions. They learned bush skills: where and how to find food, all the intricacies of their Country. They kept their Tiwi language skill and learned the songs of their Ancestors. Elaine Tiparui remembered what she used to learn when she went out every weekend:

They teach us, they teach us to go hunting, see bandicoot, where the hole is, maybe lying on the thing, logs and carpet snake. Honey honey, see the flies going round, they teach us that thing.[26]

Magdalen Kelantumama remembered the old tractor that took the girls bush on the weekend, although she remembered that the nuns came too, keeping the girls under their supervision even in the bush.[27]

Just as the girls were allowed to go 'bush' on weekends, the mission arranged for transport to take mission residents back to their Country in the school holidays. The 'outstation' or 'homelands' movement of First Nations people returning to live on Country is often associated with claims for Indigenous self-determination in the 1970s. But Tiwi (and other First Nations groups) were already

136

making these moves well before then, even in the mission heyday. Teddy Portaminni, whose own father was a leader in the later outstation movement, described the arrangement with the mission:

> So, everyone here, living here, they have no other place to go to and over the years people used to go to trucks, big truck not proper transport, trucks with seats in the back. Army truck. They drop us off … So, everyone was happy, that arrangement that we made here, the people jump on the truck, be dropped off, stay for four weeks and after four weeks, trucks come back. Then bring the people back.[28]

When the girls went bush on the weekends, there was an incentive to hurry back to the dormitory at 7 pm on a Sunday: that was movie night in the dormitory. The nuns had a projector and Tiwi men would operate it for them. No girl would miss it.[29] 'Scary' movies and 'cowboy' movies were the favourite – they loved action films. All 'cowboys and Indians' were favourites. The girls loved John Wayne too.[30] They thought he was gorgeous. Other women remembered *The Student Prince* (especially for Mario Lanza), the *Sound of Music*, *Wizard of Oz*. '*Maytime*, love story that one, love story, it's got songs that sing and make us cry.'[31] One movie in particular caught the girls' attention: *Jedda*, staring Tiwi man Robert Tudawali. Tudawali was born on Melville Island but grew up on Bagot Reserve at Darwin. He went on to become an activist for Aboriginal rights,

As they grew, the girls developed skills that served them through life. Some became nurses and worked in the hospital. James Darren Puantulua, for instance, credits his mother's skill as a nurse to the missionaries:

> [My grandmother] was working at the hospital. A lot of women, treating … teaching how to manage your own kids, and how to clean them well. How to provide good hygiene for your kids. The education came from missionary.[32]

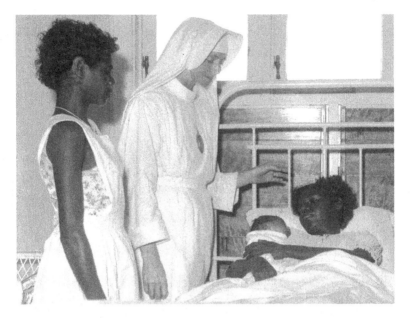

Sister Benedicta with Maggie and Annette in the hospital.
Father McMahon Collection, MSC Archives Kensington

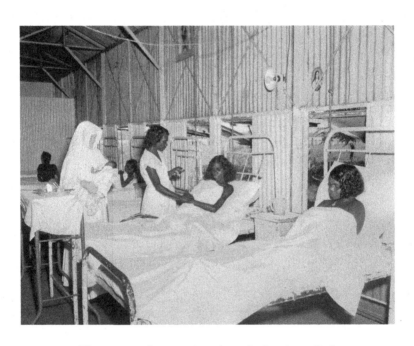

The maternity ward at the mission hospital.
National Archives of Australia, A1200, L25644

Others became teachers. Some gained administrative skills. Some became expert seamstresses and artists. Magdalen Kelantumama, therefore, praised the older women who taught the younger ones to sew and weave:

> You know in the mission days, women used to work at the thing underneath the Presbytery, they used to do sewing and teach the young ones like us. And they're good too, there's a couple of old ladies here, in their 80s, they're still alive, but they do cultural thing too. Others too, they teach us, too. I've been with those old ladies all the time. They teach kids how to do weaving and all that.[33]

Taking what they got from the missionaries – sewing – and fusing it with Tiwi cultural knowledge, they made dressmaking and printing a new way of expressing culture, and earning money. Even under the discipline and control of the mission, these women found a route for independence and cultural expression.

The cheekiness of nuns

Nuns were ever-present. The old ladies today remember how strict they were, but some of the nuns still have their deep respect. The stories are mixed. At 85, Calista Kantilla is the oldest living Tiwi woman today. She said, 'we didn't like the nuns telling us what to do'.[34] Some of them were 'cheeky' or 'a bit rough'.[35] The girls all had numbers – Calista was number 13. Sometimes the nuns used numbers in place of names. When your number was called, 'it means we were like good or bad'.[36] Some women were very positive about the experience, focusing on what they learned. Elaine Tipiloura remembered their eagerness to learn. Punishment, for her, was only being sent to do some gardening:

We get happy to go and live with the nuns, you know, go to school. And sometimes we say, when we don't think that really, we done a good job, like reading and writing. Because we weren't naughty. We just went outside and dig the garden, planted the garden, cleaned the yard in the garden. That wasn't a naughty one, you know, because we treat that way.[37]

Other Tiwi women were ambivalent about the dormitory and its discipline:

It's good. The convent strict more … because I know other women talk about it and they say, 'It was strict but not too hard, and there'd be a bit of caning'.[38]

'We used to swear at them', Calista remembered.[39] 'We'd be cheeky' too, she remembered, 'so we used to have a smack on our hand'.[40] Another woman remembered hearing how the girls learned to be strong facing the nuns:

One girl said, one of the strong women, she tell me the story, she answered that nun back. 'I can speak up', she said to that old lady. She said something back to the nun … She was strong enough to tell back, tell back to the nun … 'It's time for us to speak for our rights.' She was at the convent.[41]

Another woman spoke at length about how she resisted the nun's punishment. Her family came to defend her. Eventually, they won. The nun relented. So Tiwi people were not entirely under the missionaries' control; even the girls under the intense surveillance of the dormitory had family to defend them:

One of the nuns, I don't know why we were told to go to the convent that night and to write. I had to write this, 'I must not be disobedient'. How many times did I have to write that? It has to be one hundred. One line, 'I must not be disobedient' right up to one hundred. And every time that I found out that I couldn't go on writing it, a naughty girl I was, I'd rip the paper, squish it up and chuck it out the window.

I didn't want to go on writing it. I don't know what wrong I did, but I had to write that, 'I must not be disobedient' one line, coming down, you know, how many lines I did. But when I came down to halfway there, I said to myself, 'I can't write all the way down here'. I chuck it out. You know I was a bit cheeky and naughty in my days. Good. I rip 'em up, chuck it out.

And the time came and the sister had to come and check to see if we did that and now she's seen every one of them, they did it. When she came to me and asked me and I looked up at her and said 'did you write everything?' I told her 'nothing'. I didn't write anything. 'Oh, you're a very naughty girl. I have to get your parents tomorrow.'

That's the time when my parents came, my father. And Sister went up to him and asked him, 'what are you going to do with her and she's been very naughty'. And in those days some fathers had to smack their daughters you know, for being naughty. They had to. From their own will they had to give them a smack. That was the mission culture, but listen to my father. Now Sister went up to my father and asked him, 'now are you going to do the same things as those other men did to their children?' and my father said, 'no'. He said no. 'Why? She done a very naughty, she was very naughty.' And then he said to the nun again, 'no, I do not want to give her smack. Because I gotta give her chance, I've gotta give her one more chance. If she do it again, that's the time she will have my smack', he said.

My father was very clever to himself, he was very cheeky telling the nun off. And then he told me, 'I've gotta give you one chance, you promise you won't be naughty again', and I said I won't do it again. But then I didn't do nothing bad growing up ... I never got punished. My father won.[42]

The presence of Tiwi family watching out for each other curbed the missionaries' control. When discipline was too harsh, Tiwi people found ways to assert themselves, correcting the missionaries.

The boys' life

At this point, you might wonder what the boys were doing. Men and boys had a very different experience of the mission to women and girls. They were not subject to such intense pressure to change their lives and morals. Rather, the mission expectation seemed to be that girls would become mothers who would, in turn, influence the rising generation of boys, and therefore the girls required much stricter regulation and 'reformation'. There had been a boys' dormitory, briefly. Some boys came in as early as 1913, but the dormitory was disbanded during the Second World War. Boys stayed with their families down on the beach, while their sisters lived in the dormitory. 'We all lived on the beach', Neville Wommatakimmi remembered.[43] The houses were simple tin constructions, which the men made for their families.[44] Down by the water, they caught the sea breeze. With fishing in the afternoons, catching the sunset between the coconut fronds, life on the mission beach was idyllic.

The boys worked, mostly, with their fathers. James Darren Puantulua told of how they used to be crocodile hunters:

Me and my grandfather used to shoot crocodile. Because we've got a lot of crocodiles back home, and we shoot crocodile, and

Bathurst Island football, no date.
MSC Archives Kensington

we sell the skin to Darwin here, and get money. That was his own way of getting money, my grandfather.[45]

The boys' school was also a more relaxed affair than the girls'. They entered school at around 13 years old but only stayed a few years. Formal schooling for boys began only when Brother Howley established the boys' school in 1951: the Xavier College of today.[46] The boys were under-supported in their schooling, but not quite to the same degree. Brother Howley taught 74 boys. Howley was also the one who introduced them to their new religion: football. Today, Tiwi reminisce about playing with only a possum-skin ball on the mission grounds.

Teddy Portaminni remembered that the boys' school was strict too – especially when it came to church – but despite this, he loved it:

As for us boys, growing up in those days, you know, we, the school children had to go to mass every day. They shouldn't miss one mass. If they miss, detention ... No, I, I loved it. I liked it. I [was] always interested.[47]

While the girls were kept in the dormitory until marriage, many young men were able to travel to Darwin for work. They took off for Darwin around age 20 for apprenticeships or military service. Ted Egan spoke to us of how impressed he was with the Tiwi men he encountered in Darwin, particularly their gift at football. Tipperary had a job at the courthouse; Johnny Driver had a position at Government House. They were very professional; 'They used to dress impeccably, these Tiwi blokes'.[48]

Darwin also meant opportunities on the sporting field. Tipperary and Aloysius, together with Egan, started the St Mary's football club in Darwin in 1952 (Bishop O'Loughlin chose the strong Catholic name). Brother Pye scouted new talent from the mission, so most of the team were Tiwi.[49] They won their first Northern Territory Football League premiership in 1955. After playing for St Marty's, David Kantilla went on to become football royalty as the first Indigenous player in the South Australian League when he played for the South Adelaide Panthers in 1961.

Focusing on the family

Assimilation was different on the Tiwi Islands. Although government policy trumpeted its ambition to turn Aboriginal people into 'full citizens', the Catholic mission policy at the time did not mention citizenship or even assimilation. They continued to focus on 'protecting' Aboriginal people from 'influences outside the Reserve' and creating a community of 'civilised Christians' on their 'tribal grounds'.[50] For the Catholic missions, 'protecting' Tiwi people was about forming good Christian families.

A Tiwi family outside their house at Bathurst Island Mission, 1958.
National Archives of Australia, NAA A1200 L28045

The Commonwealth Government, meanwhile, aimed to integrate Tiwi people into the Northern Territory economy. So the mission's preference to keep Tiwi on Country (especially Tiwi women and children) exasperated the government's Welfare Branch officers to no end. They saw it as anti-assimilation and complained.[51] One welfare officer criticised the mission as attempting 'to build a wall around Bathurst Island and run it as a tribal community cloister'.[52] But the mission had no desire to send Tiwi people away from their Country, or away from the church's influence.

The suspicion between missions and government was mutual. The Catholic missions were wary of becoming entangled with secular governments; the church should not be subservient to the state. Bishop O'Loughlin actively avoided being directed by governments, refusing government capital grants because they meant he would have to furnish the government with the mission's financial statements.[53] Not only would this invite the government to meddle in church affairs, but if they accepted government money the missions would 'become too involved in material things to the detriment of the spiritual'.[54] Father McGrath was so suspicious of governments that he neglected to send records of the number of children in the dormitory to allow the mission to claim the funding. Father Henschke had to rebuke him, 'begging' him to send the information. 'The money is there & if we don't claim it, we will lose it', he wrote.[55] The mission funded capital works such as the hospital that was built in 1957 out of its own funds; its resources were very limited.[56]

Tiwi people could not know at the time, but the mission's refusal to accept government funding had a profound effect on them. There were many babies being born, but the Tiwi population on Bathurst Island was not increasing at a corresponding rate.[57] Tiwi babies were dying because the mission did not have enough clean water for a community of that size.

The Commonwealth Government began investigating the deaths. It recommended a visit from the Health Inspector to check the mission's sewerage system and dining room hygiene. All this could be solved with a proper sewerage system and enough toilets for the community. As it was, it was impossible to use fresh water for washing. The dormitory girls enjoyed year-round showers, but as the boys lived by the beach with their families, they could only shower in the wet season.[58] The Diocese of Darwin had recently commenced work on a new cathedral in Darwin; it was expensive and money was tight.[59] Nonetheless, the bishop refused to accept government funding to solve the water problem.[60] Twenty more children died at the mission in 1962; then another six died of diarrhoea between September 1962 and 1963.[61] It was finally fixed after Bishop O'Loughlin relinquished control in 1969, handing over responsibility for the Northern Territory missions to a Northern Territory Catholic Missions Council, made up of mission personnel. They accepted government support in 1971.[62]

Although the mission avoided government alliances, it did not reject assimilation altogether; instead, it wanted to make assimilation more Christian. For the Catholic missions, 'true' assimilation was about becoming part of a *Christian* community, especially taking on Catholic gender and family norms. This was why they focused so intensely on the girls.[63] Mother Marion OLSH, for example, described assimilation in terms of Catholic family life:

> So we come to the final aim of assimilation … the aboriginal
> mother to take her place side by side with other Australian
> women in the community. Can it be achieved? Almost certainly
> it can, IF we … let the seed of Christian womanhood germinate,
> grow, mature, bud, flower and bear fruit.[64]

For her, assimilation was already having an effect on missions where many Aboriginal women were 'taking their place as good wives and mothers according to Christian traditions'. She also noted that monogamy was becoming popular with young people.[65]

So the mission really did focus on the family. Ironically, perhaps, this actually had some benefits for Tiwi people. They were able to maintain a strong connection to Country and culture, even through the intensely controlled mission years. They were not exiled from their land. The mission years really did reduce violence in the community too, particularly against and over women. Calista Kantilla, for example, said:

> When I grew up I see things, because they are fighting. My dad
> was fighting too … No, but I used to run and stop him from
> fighting.[66]

But the mission, she remembered, 'tried to stop that kind of fighting'.[67] If there was ever a fight, the nuns would keep the girls in the dormitory, keeping them safe from experiencing or witnessing the violence.[68]

The nuns also regulated girls' love lives. There were to be no secret dalliances. Boys still came at night, whispering sweet nothings through the dormitory window to their girlfriends.[69] But there was always a risk the nun would catch them. The 'official' process was for boys to ask the priest for a 'ticket' with their girlfriend's name. This was effectively a licence to date:

> They used to get a ticket from priest to come down … come and see the girls … with nuns on the veranda … nuns listening and … no hugging whatever, just talk … They used to bring ticket in, ticket from father, priest.[70]

No dating without a ticket, went the rule. Marie Cecile Tipiloura talked about the punishment for breaking the dating rules:

> We don't meet men. No. Sister, she's a hard woman that nun. 'If you go with men', she put us in dormitory, shut the door. We weren't allowed to see film. Movie. We don't go to movie. Punishment for us if you go with boys.[71]

Although the mission system certainly limited girls' dating options, it also helped uphold the Tiwi kinship system during a time of rapid social change. The promise system remained resilient as parents could be sure the girls were dating no one other than their betrothed. The mission was content to co-operate with the promise system of marriage, so long as the girl's promised husband was a baptised Catholic, she was not too young (that is, she had finished school), and the man did not already have wives. Actually, the promise system provided a useful incentive (from the missionaries' perspective) to get men and boys baptised too, so long as the result was stable, monogamous Catholic families. From the Tiwi perspective, the dormitory could also help uphold Tiwi kinship rules, especially the rule that brothers and sisters do not talk to one another past childhood. Separating the boys, who stayed with their families on the beach, from the girls' dormitory also suited Tiwi. As Teresita Puruntatameri explained:

It was in Tiwi culture, when we were that age, we weren't allowed to speak to our brothers or cousin brother because that was the culture, in the culture. So our parents took us to the dormitory.[72]

But even in this regimented way, with so little contact with Tiwi boys, some of the girls found love. The women laugh and smile about it today. They were entirely naïve about the birds and the bees, but often so very in love:

They had promises. Some promise, some not, some secret love. I just got my husband![73]

I got my promise from Mum and Dad. And Mum used to come and talk to me about him. 'I don't want you to get married to other man.'[74]

[My promise] used to bring present for me [in the dormitory].[75]

We didn't know how to kiss. We just sat down and talked.[76]

I remember I had one promised old man … Mum and Dad used to tell me, 'Oh, you go to your promised husband. He said he bought you some sweet [condensed] milk'.[77]

I didn't marry my promise. I had promise, the old days, but in the end days when I was young. But I had to pick up my own whichever person that I … got a lovely husband now.[78]

The dormitory was supposed to keep the girls isolated from the temptations of the world and safe from Tiwi men. But they were not protected from all men, especially not the men inside the presbytery. Some of the priests and brothers were abusers. It is not culturally appropriate to share stories of abuse here. The Tiwi wish to heal.

That said, the dormitory girls should be recognised as the survivors they are.

The need for change

In 1954, the Bishop complained that his priests and brothers were 'ageing'. 'We are badly in need of some young blood who are strong and healthy and capable of working hard.'[79] The mental and physical strain was crushing those who remained. 'Nerves' got the better of some.[80] Bishop O'Loughlin himself admitted that the mission was 'dilapidated', and that mission staff had 'cracked under the strain'.[81] Since the mission was not sustainable, some of the priests started to wonder whether Tiwi people might be trained to take over its work. Perhaps they could be more than labourers; perhaps they could be the 'teachers, carpenters and mechanics' that would service their own community. Father Copas wrote back to Sydney with his idea:

> I have just touched upon a thesis that has been developing in
> my mind, particularly over the past 12 months. I consider that
> if the natives of New Guinea can be trained successfully as
> teachers, carpenters, mechanics etc. so also can the Aborigines
> of Australia.[82]

By the end of the 1960s, morale among the mission staff was especially low. They expected that the whole operation was in such a state of disrepair and so short of funding that the church would offload all but the spiritual work to the government. They could not keep running this small town anymore. One described the sisters and brothers as having a spirit of 'what's-it-all-worth-anyhow-as-we-are-going-to-hand-over-to-the-Government'.[83] They were giving up. Another report from one of the staff indicated that the mission was in a terrible state, but more importantly, Tiwi people had had enough of the mission's control of their lives:

Although BI [Bathurst Island] is our oldest established mission it is the worst off at present as regards living accommodation, water & sewerage, light and power, staffing. There are 900 natives – perhaps the largest concentration in the territory – who are more sophisticated than on our other missions and are becoming more demanding and difficult to handle. They have been 'kept under' for too long and not given sufficient responsibility on running their own affairs.[84]

We do not know the details of the Tiwi complaints; exactly what made them 'difficult to handle' was not written down. But, from these oral histories, we can see that Tiwi people constantly spoke up for themselves. They never yielded to the missionaries.

The missionaries underestimated the dormitory girls too. Even in that most regimented, suffocating space, they were strong. Standing together, they curbed the excesses of the mission's discipline. The girls were each other's allies; they defended each other where they could. They made the most of what they faced. When the missionaries introduced reading and writing, dressmaking, new ways to prepare food, agriculture, athletics, choirs and the intricacies of Catholic customs, the girls guzzled up the new knowledge, knowing this might all become useful. But they learned both ways. They did not neglect to learn the Tiwi language, bushcraft, Tiwi lore and the songs of their Ancestors. Like Pima before them, they were strong and made themselves strong. And when the mission left, they were ready to lead their community.

The missionaries knew they could not continue the pretence that they were masters of the Tiwi. They realised there was another option, other than handing the mission over to the government. They could hand it over to the Tiwi. In fact, some of the mission staff were starting to realise that this was precisely where they might be going wrong – handing over to Tiwi was what they needed to do. Not that they had ever truly wrested control from the Tiwi anyway.

13

THE PRIEST WHO CONVERTED

Pirrawayingi Marius Puruntatameri

I was born in 1956. And I started going to school like everyone else when I was five. It would have been in 1961. And we were taught by the Catholics, obviously. Sister Anne was the main teacher. She was really strict on us. And at that time, the missionaries wanted us to learn English only, they didn't want us to learn Tiwi.

We weren't allowed to talk Tiwi to each other during school. They stopped that, the missionaries. Because we were young, like, five, six years old, going to school, it didn't really upset us. I think the correct term to use perhaps might be we found it strange because we were young.

We wouldn't have known much English, but we thought it was strange that the missionaries would – the nuns, in particular, and the priest, obviously – would demand that we speak English only. So we found that quite strange, and maybe awkward. But we were kids, we didn't know how to get angry. We had a lot of old parents who were all good people, and they were brought up good people in positive ways and no negative things ever happened at that time. So our feelings were more positive we were all good-natured people. And we still are. So we found it strange and awkward that we were demand to speak English all the time and not Tiwi or even to practise our culture.

At that time, the policy obviously were discriminatory to

Aboriginal people, because the policy obviously wanted Aboriginal people to become like white people. This is the assimilation policy in the '50s. But when that changed, I think, it impacted on these Catholics who were told that, you know, we've got self-management, self-determination.

Around 1966, Father John Fallon was there. He was the local priest, he used to say Mass. We used to go to Mass, church service, every time on Sunday. And we got used to it. It became a habit. And people found it very interesting. And then we actually found it became normal to go to Mass. And then we learned about Jesus Christ, about God, and that was interesting. I don't think the Tiwi people thought it was a bad thing. It was, if anything else, it was strange, different. I know the assimilation policy was bad and what people done in that time in other places, killing off other Indigenous people down south, it was really bad. But up here, for some reason, Tiwi people, sort of, accepted the white fellas, if you like, coming in because they were strange – strange white fellas.

The policy was there of assimilation, you've got to turn these black fellas into good white fellas. And sadly, the missionaries went about nationally, to do that without even realising that there were consequences in that with culture.

By 1966, Father John Fallon was there for a while, he wanted to come across the strait, because he probably asked where is there the other settlement where a group of people are living. And they said, 'Yeah. The other side there', so he jumped on his tinny, it was only a 12 foot – 12 footer, 15 horsepower, came across, and we all met him. So he came and he said, 'I want to come to say Mass here'. So all the mob come around – come here so he, sort of – he just told people. And obviously at that time, there was no rejection of anything, because Tiwi people aren't bad people, they didn't know how to say 'no' to people. It's actually a good thing, because embarrassment is a big thing, people don't want to embarrass outsiders, they want to help them. And I think that's what Tiwi people are good at and are still good at helping outsiders.

Anyway, so he went and he saw some houses there where we were all living, and then he saw the Pukumani poles there. There was a few there. So he came, saw the poles, and he said, 'Hey, what are these?' and the old fellas said – including my father – they said, 'They're Pukumani poles for people that – Pukumani poles are buried around cemetery to find where the burial site is.' It's placed around the pole. And he said, 'No', he said. Father Fallon said, 'No, we're going to destroy this'.

And the old fellas, they were saying, 'No, no, no. Don't do that. Don't do that, Father, Father. No good. No good. Don't do that. What you're doing is a bad thing. No, no.' They were all calling out to him.

But he said Mass and then after Mass he walked down to the bit to where Pukumani was on, and everyone came down to see because they knew what was going to happen. And so people knew something was going to happen to the Father. And halfway across the strait, his dinghy started to sink.

And I think that was a turning point. He turned over a new leaf after that happened. He started going to the Tiwi people, said, 'Teach me Tiwi language and the culture.' Of all people, he was the first, I think, one of the first ones.

He thought about it, and thought, 'Goodness me, I've got to learn Tiwi and more about their language and culture.' I heard these old fellas, my father, and other old fellas here talking when I came here, after I left school from down south, they were talking about these priest that was wanting to learn Tiwi as well.

In everything that's happened now, the way we are, there are advantages and disadvantages. And that unfortunately the way life was and is, but sadly, the federal government had a hand in this and shaped the way things were from the late 1700s when Captain Cook came to now. Because the thinking is still there, racism is still there. Whether people accept it or not, it's still there. And it's sad, because the government really did a bad, bad thing to Indigenous people in developing these policies of assimilation.

The government needs to take responsibility for implementing the policies that they did in the '50s and before the '50s, and perhaps after. The '70s is when Gough Whitlam then started to change things. That kicked off self-empowerment and other things. A lot of the people down south, Aboriginal brothers and sisters, became involved in a lot of protests in the early '60s and '70s. And that's when things started to change.

14

CONVERTING
THE WORLD

Laura Rademaker
& Mavis Kerinaiua

Some years ago, a Tiwi woman had a vision. It was the day that her mother graduated from theological studies from Nungalinya, a college set up in the 1970s to train Aboriginal leaders to become evangelists in place of missionaries. This woman saw the Australian continent stretched out before her as the body of Christ. His feet rested down in the southern parts: Adelaide, Melbourne, Canberra, Sydney. Travelling up to Arrernte Country, his navel was at Alice Springs. His heart was Katherine – Jawoyn Country – and its river. His arms stretched out to embrace the Top End, reaching from the Gulf of Carpentaria and around to the Timor Sea. Darwin was his heart. His face was the waters to the north. He watched over travellers as they cross, giving them safe passage. And his Crown of Thorns, the glory of the continent, was, of course, the Tiwi Islands.[1] There is deep spiritual power on Tiwi Country, even as pain remains.

A lot of things changed for the Tiwi in the 1970s. Tiwi celebrate this as the time when they won back their independence. But they did not do it by turning back all the changes that had been wrought upon them. The missionaries were not banished from Tiwi Country. And Tiwi did not go back to living as they had done a century ago (although there was a mighty outstation movement and a revival of the old ceremonies). The Tiwi pressed on with new changes for their community. Instead of rejecting the past, they converted the mission to their leadership, their culture, and their priorities. They saw Christ as already being in the Country of their Ancestors, before the missionaries came, and that Country still upholds the deep truths of Tiwi lore.

At the centre of this chapter is another story many Tiwi tell, that of Father Fallon and his miraculous conversion to Tiwi culture. It's a great yarn. But it's more than that. It resonates because it speaks to the deep resilience of Tiwi lore, a lore so strong even priests, eventually, are made to accept its powerful reality. It's a story of coming to recognise and submit to Tiwi authority. It reminds us that everything and everyone on those islands, in the end, will come to see that this is Tiwi Country.

The Pukumani

Father Fallon used to talk down to Tiwi. He called Tiwi ceremony 'pagan'. 'He said that this ceremony is a pagan ceremony ... But that's not true, that was in Tiwi, Tiwi law', one woman told us.[2] Another remembered the priest 'thought we were all pagans, but we were baptised, we were Catholics'.[3] As Calista Kantilla put it, 'God gave us culture, Tiwi culture'.[4] This priest was about to learn something new.

The Tiwi are famous for their elaborate funeral ceremonies. Tiwi sing and dance for their dead. And they also create their meticulously crafted memorials: the Pukumani poles.

When someone dies, they become a marpurtiti (sometimes called 'devils' or 'ghosts' in English).[5] This spirit is invisible by day, but can be seen, faintly, in the night darkness. Marpurtiti are so light they can walk on the surface of the water.[6] They linger where the person once lived and where their body lies, but eventually, they travel onwards to the world of the marpurtiti. They can be dangerous: if lonely or upset, they can even kill. Tiwi funeral rites assist the marpurtiti to go peacefully on their journey. These rites are also incredible displays of Tiwi art, dance and music, including, famously, the Pukumani poles.

The Pukumani poles protect the dead person's spirit from bad marpurtiti,[7] as well as keeping it at the grave and comforting it. Each is unique. Its symbols reflect the dead person's spiritual identity and kinship and help carry their spirit into the world of the marpurtiti.[8] A year after the death, mourners hold a 'closing ceremony', where relatives dance and sing among the Pukumani poles. It's the largest and most important ceremony of a person's life, marking the end of their time in the world of the living.[9]

'Pukumani' also refers to the whole ritual of mourning that honours the Ancestor Beings, Purrukuparli and his son, Jirnani. Tiwi people called Purrukuparli 'the Father, creator.' [10] When Purruku-parli's son died, his rival, Japarra the Moon-Man, offered to bring the boy back to life on the third day (just as the moon 'rises' after disappearing for three days every month). But Purrukuparli refused, declaring, 'you must all follow me; as I die, so you all must die'.[11] He carried the boy's body into the water, where he joined his son in death. Purrukuparli's choice means all Tiwi follow him; all face death eventually.[12]

As the mission consolidated its presence in the Tiwi community, it put harsher restrictions on what the missionaries decided were 'pagan' elements of Tiwi culture. The generation who survived the mission era remembers this well. They still resent that they were sometimes forbidden from visiting so-called 'pagans' – their relatives who camped nearby. The women who grew up in the dormitory especially resent they were not allowed to be part of Tiwi ceremonies as schoolchildren.

But ceremony continued through the whole mission era. The annual kulama (yam) initiation ceremony, Tiwi people remember, went on in the bush without missionary interference.[13] Kulama is still important today. It enables young people to progress, year by year, through a series of ceremonial stages before entering adulthood. So it continued, even though Gsell believed that the kulama ceremony contradicted Christianity: in his view, 'they must either become pagans by undergoing initiation or Christian by receiving Baptism'.[14] Missionary Father John Fallon likewise considered the kulama a 'pagan and superstitious ceremony' as late as the 1960s and tried to get rid of it.[15] One strategy was to ensure that school and work commitments clashed with the ceremony so that Tiwi could not attend the events (as these stretch over a number of days).[16]

Missionaries were not always closed to Tiwi dance and music but sometimes attempted to harness them to teach Catholic doctrine instead. Over Christmas 1962, the missionaries encouraged a 'Corroboree Style' presentation of the Christmas story.[17] According to government bureaucrats in 1963, Bathurst Island was relatively progressive in integrating Christianity and Tiwi culture.[18] Missionaries employed Christopher 'Foxy' Tipungwuti to teach traditional dance in school.[19] It seems they thought these dances carried no real spiritual risk and could even be a vehicle of Christianisation.

But the Pukumani funeral ceremony distressed them. They had some reason to worry; Pukumani could have disturbing meanings when translated (or mistranslated) into their theological understandings. When, by the late 1960s, Tiwi people recounted the story using Christian terminology – saying, 'we shall all follow [Purrukuparli] all of us down into hell'[20] – perhaps missionaries misunderstood the Pukumani ceremonies as a rejection of the Christian heaven. A ceremony following Purrukuparli, seemingly damning all Tiwi to hell, was deeply disturbing to them.

So when anthropologist Charles Mountford visited the Tiwi Islands in 1954, he found the Pukumani ceremony under a 'complete ecclesiastical ban'.[21] Likewise, anthropologist Jane Goodale recorded that the mission gave non-Christian Tiwi people Christian funerals and buried them in the cemetery at the mission without consent. This was very upsetting for family because it meant no Pukumani could be held.[22] After her visit in the 1960s, Goodale wrote that the Pukumani ceremony was still 'virtually banned' at the mission but permitted at Snake Bay (now Milikapiti).

So Tiwi people carried on regardless of the prohibition. If someone living at the mission died, mission residents would travel to Melville Island and hold a Pukumani, away from missionaries. In fact, at every ceremony Goodale witnessed, mission residents were always present, some Catholic, participating in the rites to varying degrees.[23]

To try and stop them, Father Fallon denied Holy Communion to people who took part in Pukumani.[24] In 1968, missionaries encouraged relatives of deceased people to sign statements promising they would not hold a Pukumani ceremony.[25] By 1976, Brother John Pye wrote approvingly that the mission had caused a transition from the 'totem pole' to the Christian cross. Pye attributed the mission's success in converting the community to its refusal to accept Tiwi people as Christian converts until they had renounced their 'pagan' ceremonies. Conversion, for him, was marked by giving up Pukumani – the central ceremony in Tiwi cultural life – in favour of the cross.[26]

The conversion of the priest

All this began to change with Father Fallon's conversion. Fallon worked on Bathurst Island from 1958 until 1970. He took his final vows, becoming a priest in 1967.

'Long time, no, long time nothing'; the church did not acknowledge any connection between Tiwi culture and Catholicism, a Tiwi woman told us.[27] Tiwi influences were kept out of the church until Fallon encountered the Tiwi spiritual world.

Sometime in the 1960s, a Tiwi man named Kalikalini died. Kalikalini was avowedly not Catholic. He had refused baptism, insisting (like Purrukuparli), 'I want to go to hell'. We wonder if his audacity intimidated the missionaries.[28]

Barry Puruntatameri told us of the event that changed everything:

Some Tiwi was working with the missionary. And he saw
the big mob. He look in the bushes here … and it was on
Sunday. Sunday was big ceremony, biggest ceremony they had.
Pukumani. This Tiwi guy, he went down and he said, 'Oh, I gotta
go tell the priest'. He went down and he saw the father. He said,
'Father there is big ceremony, Pukumani in the bush'.

And he said, 'where?'

'In the bushes.'

… Everyone was dancing, clapping, everyone dancing. Few of
those men saw it, you know, Father was coming. He just walked
gently, but they didn't see him. And he was right behind them,
watching. Next thing they saw and he just bolted through
here. They all just ran out in the bush, they went and left the
ceremony. He went and threw that Pukumani, he knocked it
down, Pukumani pole.

And after that, after that, he went across to Melville and he had
an outboard motor, he was going to make Mass to the other
community, on Milikapiti. Anyway, that boat engine came out.
It went under the water. That was punishment for that.[29]

Just as the Tiwi family were dancing for Kalikalini, Fallon
intervened, knocking the Pukumani poles to the ground. There
could be no greater insult. But he received his due penalty when,
seemingly without reason, his boat began to sink.

The Old People cautioned Fallon that he was making a serious
mistake when he desecrated the ceremony. Some had already been
forewarned in a dream about what would happen.[30] As Calista
Kantilla told it:

Those Old People said to him, 'something got to be happen to you' and he came across by boat and he try start that engine then he run right in the middle of the water to stop. That engine stopped.[31]

Knowing what was to come, the Old People sat on the shore, waiting for Fallon to call for help.[32] Though the priest had done wrong, they were not angry because Fallon knew not what he did:

He came and shook the cemetery pole. The old people weren't angry, they weren't. They were sitting with spears and fighting club, but they knew it was because the mission didn't understand. So they didn't get angry.[33]

The marpurtiti (Kalikalini's spirit), disturbed by the priest's toppling of the poles, had worked some mischief, sabotaging the outboard motor (remember, marpurtiti can walk on water). Another Tiwi historian, Romolo Kantilla, told us that when the boat began to sink, the priest nearly drowned; 'that's when he called out for help. "Help! Help!"' before the Tiwi people canoed out to rescue him.[34] Fallon had no faith in Tiwi culture, so he sank down, saved only when he turned to the Tiwi.

The story continues: the offending priest saw his wrongdoing and repented. As Barry Puruntatameri explained, 'after that, maybe six months later, one year later he apologises'.[35] Tiwi people pronounced forgiveness on the repentant priest, as another Tiwi woman explained:

That priest, we always talk to him saying, 'you don't worry'. We say, 'we sorry for you' ... He said sorry to our older people. He went back, the next day he went back. 'Sorry, sorry, but I know', you know, 'God gave you your culture and like Christian way'.[36]

The priest's error was not simply disrespect, but failing to understand that this Pukumani ceremony was, for Tiwi people, not pagan but consistent with Catholic ceremony. Fallon came over and said 'you all pagan mob', but he was wrong.[37] Tiwi people had a broader vision of what could be authentically Catholic:

> He just knocked all the ceremony poles. It was very wrong because that's the culture … I don't know why, but he knocked all the poles. He wouldn't accept it. He thought we were all pagans. But we were baptised. We were Catholics.[38]

And this priest started to learn. Tiwi people taught him the meaning of ceremony and about the truths of the spiritual world. Not only did Father Fallon repent of his actions but was 'converted' to Tiwi tradition. Returning to Romolo Kantilla's account:

> They brought him back here to Bathurst and they explain to him. 'What you did back there was wrong. You shook the poles and knocked the pole over. That's why the spirit got you. What we did back there, we wasn't worshipping evil, we were having ceremony for a deceased person, a family member. That's why when you shook the poles and you got in the middle, the spirit got you.' That motor went underwater, the bung went missing. That's when he believed in our culture.[39]

Fallon's conversion was, for the Tiwi, the catalyst for a change throughout the diocese of Darwin and the broader Catholic Church. After his apology to the Tiwi, in an act of penance, he wrote to the bishop. As Barry Puruntatameri explained:

> [Fallon] write a letter to bishop: 'we should leave this cultural thing. That's their culture. They believe in their culture'. Bishop O'Loughlin, yeah, that's him.

And bishop said, 'all right'.

He came across and he apologised to all the Tiwi. The bishop apologised. He apologised to Tiwi. He said, 'I didn't know that you had a cultural, a cultural ceremony'.[40]

Archival evidence suggests that this conversation with the bishop took place over many years. In 1967, the Bishop of Darwin, JP O'Loughlin still believed that it was unlikely an Aboriginal person, 'thoroughly indoctrinated in his stone age philosophy', could ever 'make a success of life in the 20th Century'. A Tiwi man corrected him, explaining that the Tiwi had an agreement with Father Fallon that 'it was possible to follow both the European and Tiwi customs'.[41] According to Tiwi historians, Fallon also influenced the other priests and nuns, instructing them on the importance of respecting Tiwi traditions. Though Fallon went out to shake and destroy the poles, his experience, in fact 'shook' the missionaries. It made them re-think their entire mission strategy.[42]

When Fallon himself published an account of his 'conversion' to Tiwi culture in the MSC magazine in 1991, he placed it firmly in the context of the Vatican II reforms of the 1960s. The call from Rome not only to respect other cultures but to learn from them propelled a shift in missiological theory and practice. Although the council was Eurocentric, it presented opportunities for the Church to embrace cultures and approaches from beyond Europe.[43] *Nostra Aetate* (1965), for instance, taught that the Catholic Church 'rejects nothing of what is true and holy' in non-Christian religion.[44]

The immediate outcome for the Northern Territory missions was the establishment of a Mission Board in 1968, made up of priests, nuns, Aboriginal representatives and the bishop (previously the bishop alone controlled the missions).[45] This board explored a more open approach to Aboriginal cultures. For example, in the 1970s, Michael Sims of the MSC reflected that missionaries should 'study the culture' of the people they are working with and try to ensure their liturgy is 'attuned' to them.[46] Fallon not only learned to dance the Tiwi way but was part of a movement to bring the Pukumani into the church. In 1968, he arranged to install Pukumani poles in the Nguiu church; the legs of the altar would be made of six miniature poles.[47]

This conversion went all the way up to the pope. Yawuru man and former Catholic priest Patrick Dodson remembered feeling in the 1970s that the Catholic Church treated Aboriginal people as if they were inadequate, not accepting them as truly Catholic:

> There was no dialogue, never any real consideration of Aboriginal people. It was as if we were deficient … There was no dialogue, never any real consideration of being Aboriginal people.[48]

So when Pope John Paul II visited Alice Springs in 1986, his message was revolutionary. Tiwi people travelled down to Alice Springs to see him in the flesh. As one Tiwi woman explained to us:

> When pope came to Alice Springs and Darwin he said, 'Tiwi people, bring your culture into church'. That's when pope said that. That's when we bring our culture into church.[49]

His speech was groundbreaking. He seemed, for the first time, to recognise something of the significance of Country. Culture was not to be treated as a problem to be overcome, but God-given. Further, the church in Australia, he taught, needed to be converted by Aboriginal people; just as happened to Father Fallon, the rest of the Catholic Church needed to turn to listen and learn from them:

> The Church in Australia will not be fully the Church that Jesus wants her to be until [First Nations People] have made your contribution to her life and until that contribution has been joyfully received by others.[50]

The church's conversion is slow and incomplete. In 1998, the first Sorry Day in Australia, Australia's Catholic Bishops asked the Stolen Generation to forgive them.[51] For many who suffered, this is too much to ask. Many would point out that there cannot be restoration or healing without justice and truth. And there is still much work to be done, not just apologies, but reparations and empowerment for survivors. As of today, there still has never been a Tiwi priest. Tiwi have taken the Catholic faith into their lives, but it is not clear whether the Church has ever fully embraced them, and it is far from clear that it has received what they might offer it.

When Father Fallon passed away, the Tiwi danced for him, as he wanted. He was buried on the Tiwi Islands after a Catholic funeral and Pukumani dances. His burial was a mark of his belonging in the Tiwi community:

> That priest finally understood. He came back. He understood our culture and he participated too. He took part in our dancing. Even buried here in the ceremony there, Tiwi way. We danced for him too.[52]

A new era begins

Meanwhile, the spirit of change had also begun to affect First Nations policy across Australia. On 6 April 1973 Prime Minister Gough Whitlam stated that the objective of his new Aboriginal affairs policy was 'to restore to the Aboriginal people of Australia their lost power of self-determination'.[53] Christian missions to Aboriginal people were transformed into the 'communities' of today under this new federal government policy. Religious institutions were suddenly withdrawing or radically transforming their work in Aboriginal communities.[54] In the Northern Territory, the Administration's Welfare Branch was replaced with the Department of Aboriginal Affairs and hurriedly began implementing the new vision. The old mission superintendents became 'community advisers', the idea being that Aboriginal people would now make their own decisions. They would no longer be under the control of missionaries.

But, these changes had already been afoot for many years, at the urging of Tiwi people themselves. In 1971, Father Robert McKenna was saying openly that the Church needed to 'extricate itself' from the mission and hand it over to the Tiwi. He said the Tiwi were ready. When Whitlam came to power in 1973, the missionaries already knew that their days as the Tiwi 'bosses' could not continue. The Tiwi would not allow it. In July 1973, the Bishop and Catholic Missions Office agreed that the mission would be handed over to the Nguiu Council. Some missionaries would remain to assist with church, health and educational work, but Tiwi people were to be in charge.[55] The missionaries needed an exit strategy. Whitlam and his new policy provided it. As Richard Tungutalum explained:

> The government came and said, 'Tiwi mob want to run their own affairs'. So they did. We had enough, we've been under mission for a long time ... [So] they said, 'Oh, no, we want to run our own affairs'.[56]

Tiwi self-determination had already begun, in embryonic ways, even under the mission's intensive control. Today, the Tiwi are self-governing through the Tiwi Land Council and the Tiwi Islands Regional Council. The council formed through amalgamating three smaller councils in 2001 – one for Wurrumiyanga, Pirlangimpi and Milikapiti. But its roots go back to the 1960s and Tiwi agitation to take back control.

The Nguiu Tribal Council sat for the first time in 1961. On it were representatives from each of the clan groups; it fused Tiwi culture with new forms of representation and decision-making. It met weekly and made decisions on important projects such as housing and Tiwi industry.[57] There were counterpart councils in the other communities too. The missionaries, largely, were suspicious.

Researcher Colin Tatz put it tactfully: 'the mission authorities did not discourage its formation [but] they did nothing to encourage it'.[58] That is, except John Morris, a lay brother who assisted in chairing the meetings. Unordained and a volunteer, Morris did not exactly represent the church hierarchy. The council made representations to the bishop, the Administrator, Welfare Branch and politicians: the Tiwi were finding a voice.[59] Then, in 1975, Tiwi gained their own community council which could receive government funding directly. In 1978 it developed again into a community government, now with the power to make by-laws in response to local issues.[60] We spoke to a Tiwi woman who reflected on the changes since the 1960s:

> [It] is good now because the government now became shire
> council which we giving them to stand up and work, take the
> rights of the people. We've got shire council and the majority of
> them are Tiwi people and we've got white people coming as well
> to help, the work. They accept that job in the schools. We've got
> some white. And Catholic Care and the hospital.[61]

In September 1976, Tiwi demanded to form their own land council.[62] They petitioned the minister for Aboriginal affairs: 110 Tiwi signatures in all. They grounded their demands for self-governance in their eternal sovereignty and the pre-existing authority of Traditional Owners, writing that:

> There has always existed an authority exercised by what are in
> fact the traditional owners, recognised and respected by all the
> people.[63]

The formation of a Tiwi Land Council was not a government idea; it came through Tiwi political agitation. When the Tiwi Land Council formed in 1978 it was an act of Tiwi self-empowerment. Unlike others which amalgamated many language groups, the Tiwi controlled their own council, formed specifically for their interests. Membership began based on 12 clan groups on the Tiwi Islands. Some suggest the 12 followed the 12 apostles, which in turn followed the 12 tribes of Israel.[64] Its composition has varied over the years, but its core function as a way for Tiwi to govern themselves and control who comes to their land, as well as the distribution of their resources, remains.

But things are not perfect. We spoke to Tiwi leader Pirrawayingi Puruntatameri, who is on the board of the land council. He wondered whether some things might have gone backwards for Tiwi since the 1970s:

> The last 15 years, I'm 60, or maybe the last 40 years in particular, since I left school, things have changed a lot ... I always say this, and I hear a lot of people say this as well, a lot of Tiwi mob, that things have gone backwards rather than forwards. And my assumption of that is true – it is true because of the policies that have been implemented by the government. For example, in the '70s, when I finished school in '73, we came home and my family moved here to Pirlangimpi, in the '70s the council in the three major communities – the council ran our own things themselves, there was no shire council, regional council. The land council wasn't born, so the council effectively ran our own business and the community themselves. So people were empowered – they were empowered to do things ... It was really good ... Tiwi people were empowered in the '70s.[65]

Pirrawayingi's motto for the future of Tiwi is not self-determination; it's more about self-empowerment. Disappointed in governments, he sees the way forward in Tiwi developing their capacity to do things for themselves. And that is what they are doing, in education and industry.

Tiwi independence and excellence

The mission never fully handed over the school to the Tiwi; St Therese's Primary School (now Murrupurtiyanuwu Catholic School) and Xavier College in Wurrumiyanga remain controlled by the Catholic Office of Education. Many Tiwi people wanted their children to be educated in the Catholic faith, but they have also found ways to ensure this education does not neglect Tiwi cultural priorities. Many of the principals have been Tiwi, including Teresita Puruntatameri and Leah Kerinaiua (Mavis's late sister). And from the 1970s, Tiwi language was officially taught in the school. As Kerinaiua made clear, 'we believe that our Tiwi children need quality education in Tiwi language and in our traditional value and beliefs'.[66]

The bilingual program started in 1974. Those educated within it credit it with their cultural strength and knowledge today: they learned both ways. Some now worry that their children do not have the same foundation, either in Tiwi or English, as they did. As Teddy Portaminni explained:

That bilingual program was something, was a good tool for the kids here … When the bilingual program was in, there was no problem. Kids could get on and understand quickly.[67]

Former principal Teresita Puruntatameri emphasised that children found it easy to develop their English literacy once they had the opportunity to build a foundation in Tiwi:

When I became a principal it was still a bilingual school. And then about 80, I think [19]80 … the kids, they were all right writing in English. But they thought that it was something new to them. It was something that might help their English and you know, going along that path to English. And it was bilingual, all the early childhood area from preschool, transition, year one, year two, year three, that class was, they had written Tiwi but they had oral English only. Then in four, five, six, seven, fifty [per cent] was Tiwi and fifty was English. [68]

It was a shock when, in October 2008, the bilingual program was dismantled in a day:

> I heard about one [principal] … that's the school that's putting culture out. The Tiwi culture is not in the school. They have shut it down. Shut down literacy programme, bilingual, that one, in both ways education. I have been there in teacher one time … Maybe one day we'll make a trip to school and talking about it because bilingual is not there anymore. That is a big problem today.[69]

Tiwi women – the former dormitory girls who had devoted themselves to producing bilingual texts so that their children received the Tiwi-language education that they had been denied in their own youth – were insulted by the sudden cancellation of the bilingual program. Their work was dumped. The then-principal took their precious Tiwi-language booklets, primers and stories, and binned them. It was cultural vandalism. Magdalen Kelantumama found her work thrown away:

> Young people today, they can't even write in Tiwi … You know what happened back in 2009? Parliament had to stop language, speaking in our languages in the class. Know what happened to that principal here? He took all those things, translate all them other women with me, you know, all them books been thrown away … The principal took all those papers and threw it in the bin. [70]

In 2008, the first NAPLAN results for the Northern Territory revealed that remote Indigenous students were falling behind. The media saw a story. The Tiwi Islands schools found themselves the subject of a damning *Four Corners* episode that made it appear as if the children learned no English at all, rather than the truth that they learned both ways.[71] Then in October, an official report described an 'education crisis' in remote NT communities. Never mind that bilingual education was, according to the report, a 'critically important ingredient' in 'education achievement'.[72] It was too late. Bilingual education, supposedly, was the culprit. The NT education minister (herself a Tiwi woman, but not from Wurrumiyanga) announced its abolition the next day.[73] The Tiwi Land Council supported the dismantling of the project too; Tiwi do not always speak with one voice. The Catholic Education Office followed within the month.

But it's not over for Tiwi language and culture in school. 2008 also saw the establishment of Tiwi College, a private boarding school for Tiwi children, on Country, now owned and operated by the Tiwi Education Board, funded by Tiwi revenue. Tiwi took back control of their children's education. And, as always, the Tiwi are working around the confines imposed on them. Magdalen Kelantumama, for instance, declared proudly, that 'today, now, [bilingual education] came back to the class ... I'm still doing bilingual when they need me'.[74] Tiwi language and culture, increasingly, is finding its way back into the school, on the insistence of Tiwi people.

It's a similar story for Tiwi industries and businesses. After some back-and-forth between the church and Tiwi people as they navigated the new era, Tiwi established their interests. In 1971, missionaries assisted Tiwi in establishing the Nguiu Ullintjinni Association to enable the community to receive government funding for economic and social projects.[75] By the 1980s it was running the store, bank, post office, social club, film club, ferry, tourism, bakery, poultry farm, market garden, and fishing operations, all run by and for Tiwi.[76]

Back in 1969, Sister Eucharia worked with Tiwi women to start their own clothing label: Bima Wear.[77] From 1986, Tiwi women took over the management. Today it is owned and operated by Tiwi, using traditional Tiwi designs to create striking pieces of clothing. Tiwi Design started in the room underneath the old presbytery in 1968.

Bede Tungutalum and Giovanni Tipungwuti formed a partnership with the mission school's art teacher, Madeline Clear, to make early prints with wood blocks. The idea was to develop the old wood carving techniques from Pukumani poles into new artistic practices. The men soon started printing on silk screens. By 1970, they had won awards from the Industrial Design Council of Australia. Demand for Aboriginal art was soaring, so Tiwi people seized the opportunity to promote and preserve their culture and stories, as well as to grow their business.[78] In 1980, Tiwi Designs incorporated, with the objective of promoting and preserving Tiwi culture. It now employs 100 artists whose practices range from painting, sculpture, textile, ceramics, weaving and printing.

The Patakijiyali Museum came later, in the early 2000s, but is another example of Tiwi taking an opportunity and developing their independence. Sister Anne Gardiner, a nun who had been working on Tiwi Country since the 1950s, first had the idea. Now the museum displays Tiwi culture and history for tourists, but is also a keeping place for Tiwi, documenting and preserving their heritage for future generations. It fills an important cultural gap left by the bilingual program. It also provides sacramental education, but led by Tiwi. In 2017, Tiwi people took over management of the museum. And indeed, its able staff – Mavis's sister, director Fiona Kerinaiua, and museum workers Ancilla Kurrupuwu and Yvette Tipumamantumiri – have been pivotal guides and advisers for the creation of this book.

In terms of business, the eight Tiwi landowning groups came together in 2007 to establish Tiwi Enterprises and create jobs for Tiwi. It started in forestry, but quickly expanded. Now it provides accommodation and vehicle hire, freight, maintenance services, gardening, and cleaning and workshop services, as well as handling a farm and nursery and contributing to funerals and ceremonies. They are busy. Many Tiwi run their own businesses too. For example, Teddy Portaminni's Tarntipi Bush Camp, established in 2015, runs cultural education tours and camping experiences for those wishing to learn about Tiwi culture. In the words of Barry Puruntatameri, Tiwi-owned ventures are now everywhere on the Tiwi Islands:

> We've got council running it, the community and we've got different associations running their own businesses, shops, and the local Indigenous owners, they have that new shop ... that's not owned by the government or welfare or Centrelink, it's owned by this group, these people that live in this land.[79]

When it comes to the other great Tiwi faith (footy, that is), the Tiwi continue to inspire. Today you will see Anthony McDonald-Tipungwuti on the field for Essendon, Ben Rioli for South Freemantle, Maurice Rioli Jnr for Richmond and Willie 'Junior' Rioli for Port Adelaide. In recent years, Austin Wonaeamirri, Allen Christensen, Michael Long, Adam Kerinaiua, Ronnie Burns, Dean and Cyril Rioli followed their Tiwi forebears such as David Kantilla, Benny Vigona and Maurice Rioli Snr as outstanding players on the national level. Devoted to the game, the Tiwi established their own league. The Tiwi Islands Football League was established in 1968. Today it is made up of eight local clubs and the Tiwi boast the highest rate of football participation in Australia.[80] Wurrumiyanga hosts the annual grand final, attracting thousands – Tiwi and tourists – to its hallowed oval. Since 2006, Tiwi have had their own club in the Northern Territory Football League too: the famous Tiwi Bombers. As Gawin Tipiloura explained, 'Football is one way we showed everyone else that Tiwi people can be excellent, we can be the best'.[81] Given the number of Tiwi football superstars, on a per capita basis, it's clear Tiwi are the best.

Reflections on past and present

The Tiwi are plagued by the difficulties faced by many First Nations communities around Australia. The trauma of colonisation, rattling down through the generations, sometimes seems inescapable. And the Tiwi are confronting their own challenges of substance abuse, poverty, violence and despair.

When we asked Tiwi knowledge-holders about history, inevitably, they reflected on the past compared to the present. The question for many is, are things any better today? Answers are mixed. Many look back on the mission days, for instance, and remember good things. There was full employment; Tiwi were nurses, teachers and translators, labourers, mechanics, sawmillers and shop workers. No one sat around gambling. There was no alcohol or ganga then. Children went to school every day. As one woman explained, 'we had good education. We were taught properly, the proper way. We grew up learning no fighting. We're not allowed to swear. Not like this mob today'.[82] Some remember the faith and unity across clan groups; as Teddy Portaminni reminisced, 'everyone got on well together, everyone was happy. And they were full of faith, Catholic faith'.[83] But others look to Tiwi achievement since those days, their great strides of self-empowerment, and say the best days are yet to come.

For Elaine Tiparui, the mission days were happy times. They gave her generation a firm foundation from which to face present challenges. Today's problem is that the government 'took over' and made everything worse. The Tiwi need more power to control their own affairs:

I think some of the missions, like mission days, it was happy and we would go out bush with families and song, and the children. Things been change in the 70s, school was started when we start to move out [of the dormitory] and live in our parents you know … Government been change …

They were happy. We didn't have grog, nothing, then that came in … Some problems came in, that's when we got worse. I think government took over. There was good changes like, we wanted that, but I don't know if we wanted it because we didn't learn about the government law until after we learned about it. More houses and then transport, but we still had the mission days … we still had that.[84]

For James Darren Puantulua, the mission days gave Tiwi the skills they needed to manage their own affairs. He wouldn't go back to that time, but he was grateful for the legacy.

> The education came from missionary … And all that knowledge came to build a strong community. And it went like that, by doing the program. Support, like manage your own affairs, with your own family. That was what the missionary told grandmother, from grandmother to mother, our grandmother, mother, they taught us to grow up well. [85]

Walter Keriniaua Jnr, however, put it more strongly. He felt that Tiwi people were ungrateful for what the mission did:

> [the missionaries] they're the first people that helped us. They gave us this, they gave us work. 'You work, you go there.' They taught us. My great, great grandparents, even us, join in the school. And then we all like, we turn our back on them. We forget about the mission.[86]

Others did not see the mission as good for Tiwi people, even if the education was of some benefit; that benefit did not excuse the missionaries for their harsh discipline and their contempt for culture. And of course, there was also the abuse and the trauma that followed, too painful for many to put into words. Some note that a few of the missionaries, at least, apologised for the harm caused to Tiwi people and culture. As Frances Kerinaiua told us, 'they said sorry too, for what they did to us'.[87] The nuns brought care and learning, but also sometimes hurt. Yet even this was not beyond the Tiwi to forgive:

When we had that new millennium 2000, sister, she got us all the dormitory girls together, and she apologise what she done. And we didn't say anything to hurt her.[88]

Magdalen Kelantumama captured our feelings as authors best though. Her view was that the Tiwi past – both good and bad – is a source of strength. She wants Tiwi people to come to terms with what happened in their past and emphasised keeping the story strong for the next generation:

It's for kids to know what happened in the past. And we need kids to know what happened to this place, and how did the Japanese and all that. They need to tell the kids about these stories, what's happening, and their cultural stuff. Otherwise we lose everything if we don't have an older person telling stories what happened in the past. And today, they should talk about their culture and keep it strong for the next generation to come. Otherwise it will fade away.[89]

15

ON TIWI KNOWLEDGE

Teddy Portaminni

I'm one of the elders at Wurrumiyanga. I have my own small business. It's Tarntipi Homelands Aboriginal Corporation and from that I developed a camp, campsite where I, I get people in from everywhere, around Australia, around the world to come and visit me for a couple of days, maybe two or three days.

I'm a teacher. I left my teaching couple of years back, but I'm sort of still teaching in a way. I'm teaching the Tiwi way of life: the foods that we collect in the bush, the foods we collect near the waterhole there and the foods we collect in the mangroves. So, we go down there and we, we collect crabs, or maybe if we're lucky enough, we find a tree with plenty of mangrove worm.

I've come to realise that I've a lot to offer, a lot to give. I remember that I've got something for myself which I can give – that something came from the old people who looked after me when I was a kid, you know, learning.

When I was a little boy, The priest would say 'hey. You are pagan people, you shouldn't practise'. But we said, 'No, no, no this is our way. This is ours. You can't tell us stop'.

And that's what's happening now, because a lot of white people are saying, stop. 'Stop what you're doing. This is new. You've got to follow this. Follow our way.' No, no. We are Tiwi.

The Old People and my people who are same age, that grew up with the mission, we weren't happy that the missions are going away, but we still have what they've brought here. We still have that and we're glad that they brought it for us and gave it to us. That's something, another thing we pass on too. We've got our culture and that Catholic faith. We've got to keep going with that for our kids.

For, for me, going away, looking at different things, talking to different people, meeting different people from other countries make me think, how can I tell these people who I am? It's important for them to know, because I've got something there which I can show these people. I believe it's important for us to keep it, keep our language and culture, custom and belief and everything associated within the Tiwi society. We really need to honour it. So I own what I own and will not let anybody get what I have, because it's only for me, to share with people like you or, or the young people coming up.

APPENDIX: TIWI FOOTBALL LEGENDS

Below are the names of many of the outstanding Tiwi footballers over the generations. This list is not comprehensive (it was simply not possible to include the full breadth and details of Tiwi achievement), but it reflects the consistent Tiwi excellence over the decades.

Player	Clubs and Honours
Cyril Rioli Snr (1934–2014)	St Mary's (NTFL)
David Kantilla (1938–1978)	St Mary's (NTFL), South Adelaide (SANFL) Northern Territory Hall of Champions, Indigenous Team of the Century
Bertram Kantilla	St Mary's and Waratahs (NTFL) Nichols Medal
Sebastian Rioli (1954–2012)	South Freemantle (WAFL)
Maurice Rioli Snr (1957–2010)	South Freemantle (WAFL), Richmond (AFL) Norm Smith Medal, WAFL Hall of Fame, Indigenous Team of the Century
Benny Vigona (1958)	South Freemantle (WAFL)
John Rioli	South Freemantle (WAFL) Jack Clarke Medal
Michael Long (1969)	St Mary's (NTFL), Essendon (AFL). Norm Smith Medal, Northern Territory Hall of Champions, Australian Football Hall of Fame, Indigenous Team of the Century
William John 'Willie' Rioli Snr (1972–2022)	St Marys (NTFL), South Freemantle (WAFL), Hawthorn (AFL) Nichols Medal

Player	Clubs and Honours
Ronnie Burns (1973)	Geelong and Adelaide (AFL)
Adam Kerinaiua (1974)	Brisbane (AFL)
Dean Rioli (1978)	Essendon (AFL)
Cyril Rioli Jnr	St Mary's (NTFL), South Freemantle (WAFL) Nichols Medal
Shane 'Tippa' Tipuamantamerri (1981)	Tiwi Bombers (NTFL), South Freemantle (WAFL), Glenelg (SANFL) Nichols Medal
Malcolm Lynch (1988)	Western Bulldogs (AFL)
Austin Wonaeamirri (1988)	St Mary's (NTFL), Melbourne (AFL)
Cyril 'Junior Boy' Rioli (1989)	St Mary's (NTFL), Hawthorn (AFL) Norm Smith Medal
Allen Christensen (1991)	Brisbane and Geelong (AFL)
Anthony 'Wala' McDonald-Tipungwuti (1993)	Tiwi Bombers (NTFL), Essendon (AFL)
Ben Rioli (1993)	St Mary's (NTFL), South Freemantle (WAFL)
Willie 'Junior' Rioli (1995)	Glenelg (SANFL), West Coast and Port Adelaide (AFL)
Jake Long (1996)	Essendon (AFL)
Ben Long (1997)	St Kilda and Gold Coast (AFL)
Kim Kantilla	South Adelaide (SANFL)
Brendan Gleeson Kerinaiua (Kantilla)	Tiwi Bombers (NTFL)
Maurice Rioli Jnr (2002)	Richmond (AFL)
Anthony Munkara (2004)	Tiwi Bombers (NTFL), West Adelaide (SANFL), Essendon (AFL)

REFERENCES

Archival collections

Australian Institute of Aboriginal and Torres Strait Islander Studies (AIATSIS), Canberra
Australian War Memorial (AWM), Canberra
Missionaries of the Sacred Heart (MSC) Archives, Sydney
Mitchell Library (ML), Sydney
National Archives of Australia (NAA), Canberra, Darwin
Northern Territory Archives Service (NTAS), Darwin
Pitt Rivers Museum, Oxford

Newspapers

Advertiser, Adelaide
Advocate, Melbourne
Age, Melbourne
Annals of Our Lady of the Sacred Heart, Sydney
Australian Annals, Sydney
Cairns Post, Cairns
Catholic Press, Sydney
Courier-Mail, Brisbane
Kalgoorlie Miner, Kalgoorlie
Mail, Adelaide
Morning Bulletin, Rockhampton
New Zealand Tablet, Dunedin
Northern Standard, Darwin
Sydney Morning Herald, Sydney
Transcontinental, Port Augusta

Oral histories

Barry Puruntatameri, oral history interview with authors, 9 September 2016.
Bede Tungutalum, oral history interview with authors, 31 August 2016.
Bernard Tipiloura, oral history interview with authors, 20 June 2016.
Calista Kantilla, oral history interview with authors, 1 September 2016.
Calista Kantilla, oral history interview with authors, 23 March 2022.
Dulcie Kelantumama, oral history interview with authors, 9 June 2016.

Elaine Tiparui, oral history interview with authors, 31 August 2016.
Enid Cunningham, oral history interview with Laura Rademaker, 6 September 2016.
Frances Kerinaiua, oral history with authors, 11 June 2016.
Francillia Puruntatameri, oral history interview with authors, 23 March 2022.
Henrietta Hunter, oral history with authors, 19 November 2015.
James Darren Puantulura, oral history interview with authors, 24 March 2022.
Karen Tipiloura, oral history with authors, 23 March 2022.
Kerryann Kerinaiua, oral history interview with authors, 26 March 2022.
Magdalen Kelantumama, oral history with authors, 28 March 2022.
Marie Cecile Tipiloura, oral history interview with authors, 8 June 2016.
Mavis Kerinaiua, oral history interview with Laura Rademaker, 19 June 2016.
Murabuda Wurramarba, oral history with Laura Rademaker, 10 December 2012.
Neville Wommatakimmi, oral history interview with authors, 26 March 2022.
Pirrawayingi, oral history with authors, 5 September 2016.
Richard Tungutalum, oral history interview with authors, 2 September 2016.
Romolo Kantilla, oral history interview with authors, 22 November 2015.
Teddy Portaminni, oral history interview with authors, 26 March 2022.
Teresita Puruntatameri, oral history interview with authors, 23 November 2015.
Walter Kerinaiua Jnr, oral history interview with authors, 24 March 2022.

Bibliography

Address of John Paul II to the Aborigines and Torres Strait Islanders in Blatherskite Park, Alice Springs, 29 November 1986, Available online: <w2.vatican.va/content/john-paul-ii/en/speeches/1986/november/documents/hf_jp-ii_spe_19861129_aborigeni-alice-springs-australia.html>.
Adepoyibi, Adeniba C. *The Development of Responsibility and Management of Aboriginal Community Councils in East Arnhem Land and the Tiwi Islands.* Charles Darwin University (Australia), 1999.
Anderson, Warwick. *Colonial Pathologies: American Tropical Medicine, Race, and Hygiene in the Philippines,* Durham: Duke University Press, 2006.
Assimilation for Our Aborigines (Canberra: Govt. Printer, 1958).
Austin-Broos, Diane. 'The anthropology of conversion', in A Buckser and S Glazier (eds.), *The Anthropology of Religious Conversion*, 1–12, Lanham: Rowman & Littlefield, 2003.
Austin-Broos, Diane. *Arrernte Present, Arrernte Past: Invasion, Violence, and Imagination in Indigenous Central Australia.* Chicago: University of Chicago Press, 2009.
Brandl, Maria. 'Pukumani: The Social Context of Bereavement in a North Australian Aboriginal Tribe', PhD Thesis, University of Western Australia, 1971.
Brock, Peggy et al. *Indigenous Evangelists and Questions of Authority in the British Empire, 1750–1940.* Boston: Brill, 2015.
Campbell, Genevieve. 'Ngarukuruwala – We Sing: The Songs of the Tiwi Islands, Northern Australia', PhD Thesis, University of Sydney, 2013.
Campbell, John. *Geographical Memoir of Melville Island and Port Essington on the Cobourg Peninsula, Northern Australia: With Some Observations on the Settlements Which Have Been Established on the North Coast of New Holland.* London: Royal Geographical Society, 1834.

Caruana, Anthony. *Monastery on the Hill: A History of the Sacred Heart Monastery, Kensington 1897–1997.* Kensington: Nelen Yubu Missiological Unit, 2000.

Clarke, Anne. 'Winds of Change: An Archaeology of Contact in the Groote Eylandt Archipelago, Northern Australia', PhD thesis, Australian National University, 1994.

Collier, Jane. *Marriage and Inequality in Classless Societies.* Stanford, California: Stanford University Press, 1993.

Comaroff, Jean. 'Missionaries and Mechanical Clocks: An Essay on Religion and History in South Africa', *The Journal of Religion*, 71, No. 1 (1991): 1–17.

Coon, Carleton. *The Origin of Races.* New York: Knopf, 1962.

Crawford, Sue. 'Spears to Crosses: An Anthropological Analysis of the Social Systems of Missionaries in Northern Australia', Honours Thesis, Australian National University, 1978.

Cuskelly, EJ. *Jules Chevalier: Man with a Mission*, Rome: Casa Generaliziz Missionari Del Sacro Cuore, 1975.

Daughters of Our Lady of the Sacred Heart. *Constitutions of the Daughters of Our Lady of the Sacred Heart*, Sydney, 1928.

Declaration on the relation of the Church to non-Christian religions, Nostra Aetate, proclaimed by Pope Paul VI, 28 October 1965.

Deverell, Garry J. *Gondwana Theology: A Trawloolway Man Reflects on Christian Faith.* Morning Star Publishing, 2018.

Dodson, Patrick, Jacinta Elston and Brian McCoy. 'Leaving Culture at the Door: Aboriginal Perspectives on Christian Belief and Practice', *Pacifica: Australasian Theological Studies* 19, no. 3 (2006): 249–262.

Egan, Ted and Bill Gammage. *Ted Egan Interviewed by Bill Gammage [Sound Recording]*, 2003.

Ennis, Henry. *Remarks on Board His Majesty's Ship Tamar: In a Voyage from England to Port Praia, Cape of Good Hope, New South Wales, and from Thence Along the Coast of Australia, to Port Essington in the Cobourg Peninsula, and Thence to Bathurst and Melville Islands, Apsley's Straits, Between 27th February & the 13th of November 1824; and Continued in the Ship Countess of Harcourt, to the Isle of France, to 7th February 1825.* South Melbourne, Victoria; Richard Griffin Publisher Pty Ltd, 1983.

Evans, Nicholas. 'Review Article: Australian Languages Reconsidered: A Review of Dixon (2002)', *Oceanic Linguistics*, 44, No. 1 (2005): 242–286.

Eves, Richard. 'Going Troppo: Images of White Savagery, Degeneration and Race in Turn-of-the-Century Colonial Fictions of the Pacific', *History and Anthropology*, 11, No. 2–3 (1999): 351–385.

Fallon, John. 'The Good Old Days', *Nelen Yubu*, Vol. 48 (1991).

Farram, Steven. 'The Tiwi of Melville Island, the Portuguese of Timor, and Slavery.' *Bijdragen tot de taal-, land-en volkenkunde*, 178 (2022): 5–37.

Forrest, Peter and Sheila Forrest. *Tiwi Meet the Future: Ngawurraningimarri: All Come Together.* Winnellie: Tiwi Land Council, 2005.

Fredericksen, Clayton. 'Confinement by Isolation: Convict Mechanics and Labour at Fort Dundas, Melville Island', *Australasian Historical Archaeology*, 19 (2001): 48–59.

Fry, Henry. 'A Bathurst Island Mourning Rite', *Mankind*, 4, No. 2 (1949).

Ganter, Regina. '"Australia Seemed Closer than Tokyo": Japanese Labourers in Australia, 1870s to 1940s', D Grant and G Seal (eds.), *Australia in the World: Perceptions and Possibilities.* Perth: Black Swan Press, 1994.

Ganter, Regina. 'Bathurst Island Mission', *German Missionaries in Australia*, Griffith University (2009–2018). Available online: <missionaries.griffith.edu.au/>.

Girola, Stefano. 'Rhetoric and Action: The Policies and Attitudes of the Catholic Church with Regard to Australia's Indigenous Peoples, 1885–1967', PhD thesis, University of Queensland (2006).

Gondarra, Dyiniyini. *Father, You Gave Us the Dreaming*, Darwin: Uniting Church in Australia, 1988.

Gondarra, Dyiniyini. *Series of Reflections of Aboriginal Theology*, Darwin: Uniting Church in Australia, 1986.

Goodale, Jane. '"Taramaguti" Today: Changing Roles of Senior Tiwi Wives as Household Managers', *Pacific Studies*, 19, No. 4 (1996): 131–154.

Goodale, Jane. *Tiwi Wives: A Study of the Women of Melville Island, North Australia*. Seattle: University of Washington Press, 1971.

Grau, Andree. 'Dreaming, Dancing, Kinship: The Study of Yoi, the Dance of the Tiwi of Melville and Bathurst Islands, North Australia', PhD Thesis, Queen's University, 1983.

Gray, Geoffrey. 'The Army Requires Anthropologists: Australian Anthropologists at War, 1939–1946', *Australian Historical Studies*, 37, No. 127 (2006): 156–180.

Gsell, Francis Xavier. *'The Bishop with 150 Wives': Fifty Years as a Missionary*. Sydney: Angus and Robertson, 1955.

Hall, Robert A. *The Black Diggers*. Canberra: Aboriginal Studies Press, 1997.

Harris, Alana. *Faith in the Family: A Lived Religious History of English Catholicism, 1945–1982*. Oxford: Oxford University Press, 2016.

Hart, Charles William Merton. 'The sons of Turimpi', *American Anthropologist*, 56, No. 2 (1954): 242–261.

Haultain, Charles Theodore Graham. *Watch Off Arnhem Land*. Canberra: Roebuck Society, 1971.

Heere, JE (ed.), *The Part Borne by the Dutch in the Discovery of Australia 1606–1765*, translated by C Stoffel. London: Luzac, 1899.

Henry, Richard. *Early Voyages to Terra Australis, Now Called Australia: A Collection of Documents, and Extracts from Early Manuscript Maps, Illustrative of the History of Discovery on the Coasts of That Vast Island, from the Beginning of the Sixteenth Century to the Time of Captain Cook*. London: Hakluyt Society, 1859.

Jonas, Raymond. *France and the Cult of the Sacred Heart: An Epic Tale for Modern Times*. Berkeley: University of California Press, 2000.

Jones, Timothy Willem. 'The Missionaries' Position: Polygamy and Divorce in the Anglican Communion, 1888–1988', *Journal of Religious History*, 35, Issue 3, (2011): 393–408.

Kenny, Robert. *The Lamb Enters the Dreaming: Nathanael Pepper & the Ruptured World*. Melbourne: Scribe, 2010.

King, Phillip Parker. *Narrative of a Survey of the Intertropical and Western Coasts of Australia Performed between the Years 1818 and 1822*, 1. London: John Murray, 1826.

Love, JRB. *The Aborigines: Their Present Condition as Seen in Northern South Australia, the Northern Territory, North-West Australia and Western Queensland*. Melbourne: Board of Missions of the Presbyterian Church of Australia, 1915.

Low, Gail Ching-Liang. 'White Skins/Black Masks: The Pleasures and Politics of Imperialism', *New Formations*, 9 (1989): 83–103.

Magowan, Fiona. *Melodies of Mourning: Music & Emotion in Northern Australia*. Crawley: University of Western Australia Press, 2007.

Massam, Katharine. *Sacred Threads: Catholic Spirituality in Australia, 1922–1962*. Kensington: UNSW Press, 1996.

McDonald, Heather. 'Universalising the Particular? God and Indigenous Spirit Beings in East Kimberley', *Australian Journal of Anthropology*, 21, Issue 1 (2010): 51–70.

McGrath, Ann. 'Consent, Marriage and Colonialism: Indigenous Australian Women and Colonizer Marriages', *Journal of Colonialism and Colonial History*, 6, No. 3 (2005).

Merlan, Francesca. *Dynamics of Difference in Australia: Indigenous Past and Present in a Settler Country*, Philadelphia: University of Pennsylvania Press, 2018.

Morphy, Howard and Frances Morphy. 'The "Myths" of Ngalakan History: Ideology and Images of the Past in Northern Australia', *Man*, 19, No. 3 (1984): 459–478.

Morris, John. 'Continuing "Assimilation"?: A Shifting Identity for the Tiwi 1919 to the Present', PhD Thesis, University of Ballarat, 2003.

Morris, John. 'Memories of the Buffalo Shooters: Joe Cooper and the Tiwi (1895–1936)', *Aboriginal History*, Vol. 24, (2000): 141–152.

Morris, John. 'Potential Allies of the Enemy: The Tiwi in World War Two', *Journal of Northern Territory History*, No. 15 (2004): 77–90.

Morris, John. 'The Japanese and the Aborigines: An Overview of the Efforts to Stop the Prostitution of Coastal and Island Women', *Journal of Northern Territory History*, No. 21 (2010): 15–36.

Morris, John. 'The Tiwi and the British: An Ill-Fated Outpost', *Aboriginal History*, 25, (2001): 243–261.

Morris, John. *The Tiwi: From Isolation to Cultural Change: A History of Encounters Between an Island People and Outside Forces*, Darwin: Northern Territory University Press, 2001.

Munkara, Marie. *Every Secret Thing*. St Lucia: University of Queensland Press, 2009.

Munkara, Marie. *Of Ashes and Rivers That Run to the Sea*. Random House Australia, 2016.

Murray, Frances. 'The Development of Successful Bilingual, Biliterate and Bicultural Pedagogy: Place for Tiwi Teachers and Tiwi Language in Learning', in *History of Bilingual Education in the Northern Territory*. Springer, 2017.

Northern Territory Emergency Response. 'Northern Territory Emergency Response: Report of the NTER Review Board', Canberra: Australian Government, 14 October 2008.

O'Carrigan, John and John Morris. 'Christian Marriage and Family Life on Bathurst Island', *Arnhem Land Epistle*, October 1964.

O'Malley, JW. *What Happened at Vatican II*. Cambridge, Mass, Harvard University Press, 2010.

Orsi, Robert. *Between Heaven and Earth: The Religious Worlds People Make and the Scholars Who Study Them*. Princeton: Princeton University Press, 2005.

Pattel-Gray, Anne. *Aboriginal spirituality: Past, present, future*. Blackburn: Harper Collins, 1996.

Paulson, Graham. 'Towards an Aboriginal Theology', *Pacifica*, 19, No. 3 (2006): 310–320.

Phillip P, King. *Narrative of a Survey of the Intertropical and Western Coasts of Australia: Performed Between the Years 1818 and 1822*. London: John Murray, 1826.

Pilling, Arnold. 'A Historical versus a Non-Historical Approach to Social Change and Continuity among the Tiwi', *Oceania* 32, no. 4 (1962): 321–326.

Portelli, Alessandro. *The Death of Luigi Trastulli and Other Stories: Form and Meaning in Oral History*. Norwell: Kluwer, 1991.

Pugh, Derek. *The British in North Australia: Fort Dundas 1824–29*, Rapid Creek: Derek Pugh, 2017.

Pye, John. *The Tiwi Islands*. Nguiu: Wurrumiyanga, 1977.

Rademaker, Laura. 'An Emerging Protestant Doctrine of Self-Determination in the Northern Territory' in *Indigenous Self-Determination in Australia: Histories and Historiography*, edited by Laura Rademaker and Tim Rowse, 1–36. Canberra: Australian National University Press, 2020.

Rademaker, Laura and Tim Rowse. 'How Shall We Write the History of Self-Determination in Australia?' in *Indigenous Self-Determination in Australia: Histories and Historiography*, edited by Laura Rademaker and Tim Rowse, 1–36. Canberra: Australian National University Press, 2020.

Rainbow Spirit Elders. *Rainbow Spirit Theology: Towards an Australian Aboriginal Theology*. Hindmarsh: AFT Press, 1997.

Rambo, Lewis. *Understanding Religious Conversion*. New Haven: Yale University Press, 1993.

Riseman, Noah. 'Contesting White Knowledge: Yolngu Stories from World War II', *The Oral History Review*, 37, Issue 2 (2010): 170–190.

Riseman, Noah. *Defending Whose Country?: Indigenous Soldiers in the Pacific War*. Lincoln: University of Nebraska Press, 2012.

Rogers, Charlotte. *Jungle Fever: Exploring Madness and Medicine in Twentieth-Century Tropical Narratives*. Vanderbilt University Press, 2012.

Rowse, Tim. *White Flour, White Power: From Rations to Citizenship in Central Australia*. Cambridge: Cambridge University Press, 1998.

Shanks, G Dennis et al. 'Extreme Mortality After First Introduction of Measles Virus to the Polynesian Island of Rotuma, 1911', *American Journal of Epidemiology*, 173, Issue 10 (2011): 1211–1222.

Shellam, Tiffany. *Shaking Hands on the Fringe: Negotiating the Aboriginal World at King George's Sound*. Crawley: UWA Press, 2009.

Shulman, Stanford T, Deborah L Shulman, and Ronald H Sims. 'The Tragic 1824 Journey of the Hawaiian King and Queen to London History of Measles in Hawaii', *Pediatric Infectious Disease Journal*, 28, No. 8 (2009): 728–733.

Simpson, Jane, Jo Caffery, and Patrick McConvell. *Gaps in Australia's Indigenous Language Policy: Dismantling Bilingual Education in the Northern Territory*, AIATSIS Discussion Paper Number 24, 2009, 25–26.

Sleeper-Smith, Susan. 'Women, Kin, and Catholicism: New Perspectives on the Fur Trade', *Ethnohistory*, 47, No. 2 (2000): 423–452.

Stockton, Eugene. 'Maverick Missionaries: An Overlooked Chapter in the History of Catholic Missions', Tony Swain and Deborah Bird Rose (eds), *Aboriginal Australians and Christian Missions: Ethnographic and Historical Studies*, 201–210. Adelaide: Australian Association for the Study of Religions, 1988.

Tatz, Colin. 'Aboriginal Administration in the Northern Territory of Australia', PhD Thesis, Australian National University, 1964.

Therese of Lisieux. *Story of a Soul: The Autobiography of St. Therese of Lisieux: Third Edition Translated from the Original Manuscripts*. Washington, DC: Institute of Carmelite Studies Publications, 2013.

Tiwi Heroes: World War Two Encounters, NT Library exhibition, March 2022.

Tiwi Land Council. 'Land Ownership', Available online: <tiwilandcouncil.com/index.cfm?fuseaction=page&p=228&l=2&id=60&smid=116>.

Tungutalum, Geraldine. *Ngirramini Ngini Japarra Amintiya Purrukuparli*, Nguiu: Nguiu Nginingawila Literature Production Centre, 1988.

Tweed, Thomas. *Crossing and Dwelling: A Theory of Religion*. Cambridge, Mass: Harvard University Press, 2009.

Urry, James and Michael Walsh. 'The Lost "Macassar Language" of Northern Australia', *Aboriginal History*, Vol. 5 (1981): 91–108.

Venbrux, Eric. *A Death in the Tiwi Islands: Conflict, Ritual and Social Life in an Australian Aboriginal Community*. Cambridge: Cambridge University Press, 1995.

Venbrux, Eric. 'Property Rights and Tourism in the Tiwi Islands, Northern Australia', *Property Rights & Economic Development*, 2012.

Venbrux, Eric. 'The Post-colonial Virtue of Aboriginal Art', *Zeitschrift Für Ethnologie*, 2002.

Venbrux, HJM. 'Indigenous Religion in an Intercultural Space', L Zimmer-Tamakoshi and J Dickerson-Putman (eds.), *Pulling the Right Threads: The Ethnographic Life and Legacy of Jane C Goodale*, 168–186. Chicago: University of Illinois Press, 2008.

Watson Frederick (ed.), *Historical Records of Australia*. Sydney: Government Printer, 1922, Series 3, Vol. 5.

White, Sophie. *Wild Frenchmen and Frenchified Indians: Material Culture and Race in Colonial Louisiana*. Philadelphia: University of Pennsylvania Press, 2013.

Whitehouse, Harvey. 'Appropriated and monolithic Christianity in Melanesia', in Fenella Cannel (ed.), *The Anthropology of Christianity*. Durham: Duke University Press, 2006.

Wilson, Rob. *Be Always Converting, Be Always Converted: An American Poetics*. Cambridge, Mass: Harvard University Press 2009.

Wilson, Thomas Braidwood. *Narrative of a Voyage Round the World: Comprehending an Account of the Wreck of the Ship "Governor Ready" in Torres Straits; a Description of the British Settlements on the Coasts of New Holland, More Particularly Raffles Bay, Melville Island, Swan River, and King George's Sound; Also to Manners and Customs of the Aboriginal Tribes*. London: Gilbert & Piper, 1835.

Yengoyan, Aram. 'Religion, Morality, and Prophetic Traditions: Conversion Among the Pitjantjatjara of Central Australia', in R Hefner (ed.), *Conversion to Christianity: Historical and Anthropological Perspectives on a Great Transformation*, 233–258. Berkeley: University of California Press, 1993.

NOTES

2 Turning around

1   Francis Xavier Gsell, *'The Bishop with 150 Wives': Fifty Years as a Missionary* (Sydney: Angus and Robertson, 1955), 78, 90.

2   Gsell, *'The Bishop with 150 Wives'*, 90. MSC Archives Kensington, 'Bathurst Island 9', 'Index Bishop Gsell's Wives'. See also John Arnold Morris, *The Tiwi: From Isolation to Cultural Change: A History of Encounters Between an Island People and Outside Forces* (Darwin: Northern Territory University Press, 2001), 119.

3   Gsell, *'The Bishop with 150 Wives'*, 83–90.

4   Timothy Willem Jones, 'The Missionaries' Position: Polygamy and Divorce in the Anglican Communion, 1888–1988', *Journal of Religious History*, Vol. 35, Issue 3 (2011), 399.

5   86.8 per cent of residents on the Tiwi Islands identified as Christian; this includes the 78.3 per cent who identified as Roman Catholic. Tiwi Islands, 2021 Census Community Profile, < www.abs.gov.au/census/find-census-data/quickstats/2021/702031060>.

6   Lewis Rambo, *Understanding Religious Conversion* (New Haven: Yale University Press, 1993), 3.

7   Thomas Tweed, *Crossing and Dwelling: A Theory of Religion* (Cambridge, Mass: Harvard University Press, 2009), 167; Rob Wilson, *Be Always Converting, Be Always Converted: An American Poetics* (Cambridge, Mass: Harvard University Press 2009), 3.

8   Diane Austin-Broos, 'The anthropology of conversion', in A Buckser and S Glazier (eds.), *The Anthropology Of Religious Conversion* (Lanham: Rowman & Littlefield, 2003), 2–5.

9   The 'salvage' approach was led by Franz Boas and in Australian anthropology included Norman Tindale and Alfred Radcliffe-Brown.

10   Aram Yengoyan, 'Religion, Morality, and Prophetic Traditions: Conversion among the Pitjantjatjara of Central Australia', in R Hefner (ed.), *Conversion to Christianity: Historical and Anthropological Perspectives on a Great Transformation* (Berkeley: University of California Press, 1993), 234–236.

11   Dyiniyini Gondarra, *Father, You Gave us the Dreaming* (Darwin: Uniting Church in Australia, 1988); Anne Pattel-Gray, *Aboriginal spirituality: Past, present, future* (Blackburn: Harper Collins, 1996); Rainbow Spirit Elders, *Rainbow Spirit Theology: Towards an Australian Aboriginal Theology* (Hindmarsh: AFT Press, 1997), 16, 38; Dyiniyini Gondarra, *Series of Reflections of Aboriginal Theology* (Darwin: Uniting Church in Australia, 1986), iv. Garry J Deverell, *Gondwana Theology: A Trawloolway Man Reflects on Christian Faith* (Morning Star Publishing, 2018). Graham Paulson, 'Towards an Aboriginal Theology', *Pacifica*, Vol. 19, No. 3 (2006), 310–20.

12   Diane Austin-Broos, *Arrernte Present, Arrernte Past: Invasion, Violence, and Imagination in Indigenous Central Australia* (Chicago: University of Chicago Press, 2009), 21–22. Heather McDonald, 'Universalising the Particular? God and Indigenous Spirit Beings in East Kimberley', *TAJA*, Vol. 21, Issue 1 (2010) 51, 64;

Fiona Magowan, *Melodies of Mourning: Music & Emotion in Northern Australia* (Crawley: University of Western Australia Press, 2007), 184; Robert Kenny, *The Lamb Enters the Dreaming: Nathanael Pepper & the Ruptured World* (Melbourne: Scribe, 2010).

13 Peggy Brock et al., *Indigenous Evangelists and Questions of Authority in the British Empire, 1750–1940,* (Boston: Brill, 2015), 117–131, 191–94.

14 Gondarra, *Series of Reflections*, 26.

15 Harvey Whitehouse, 'Appropriated and monolithic Christianity in Melanesia', in Fenella Cannel (ed.), *The Anthropology of Christianity* (Durham: Duke University Press, 2006), 296.

16 Daughters of Our Lady of the Sacred Heart, *Constitutions of the Daughters of Our Lady of the Sacred Heart* (Sydney, 1928), 7.

17 Alessandro Portelli, *The Death of Luigi Trastulli and Other Stories: Form and Meaning in Oral History,* (Norwell: Kluwer, 1991), 2.

18 Robert Orsi, *Between Heaven and Earth: The Religious Worlds People Make and the Scholars Who Study Them* (Princeton: Princeton University Press 2005), 2, 18.

19 Geraldine Tungutalum, *Ngirramini Ngini Japarra Amintiya Purrukuparli* (Nguiu: Nguiu Nginingawila Literature Production Centre, 1988).

3   Just like Captain Cook
1 Tampuwu is also spelled 'Tampu' or 'Tambu' in some sources.

4   Turning trespassers
1 Carleton Coon, *The Origin of Races* (New York: Knopf, 1962), 98.

2 Nicholas Evans, 'Review Article: Australian Languages Reconsidered: A Review of Dixon (2002)', *Oceanic Linguistics*, Vol. 44, No. 1 (2005), 256.

3 Enid Cunningham, oral history interview with Laura Rademaker, 6 September 2016.

4 Eric Venbrux, *A Death in the Tiwi Islands: Conflict, Ritual, and Social Life in an Australian Aboriginal Community* (Cambridge: Cambridge University Press, 1995), 39.

5 Romolo Kantilla, oral history interview with authors, 22 November 2015.

6 Anne Clarke, 'Winds of Change: An Archaeology of Contact in the Groote Eylandt Archipelago, Northern Australia', PhD thesis, Australian National University (1994), 14.

7 Clarke, 'Winds of Change', 14; James Urry and Michael Walsh, 'The Lost "Macassar Language" of Northern Australia', *Aboriginal History*, Vol. 5 (1981), 94–95.

8 John Pye, *The Tiwi Islands* (Kensington, New South Wales: [Brother J Pye], 1977), 7.

9 Barry Puruntatameri, oral history interview with authors, 9 September 2016.

10 Bede Tungutalum, oral history interview with authors, 9 September 2016.

11 Farram, Steven. 'The Tiwi of Melville Island, the Portuguese of Timor, and Slavery.' *Bijdragen tot de taal-, land-en volkenkunde* 178 (2022), 5–37.

12 Phillip Parker King, *Narrative of a Survey of the Intertropical and Western Coasts of Australia Performed Between the Years 1818 and 1822*, Vol. 1 (London: John Murray, 1826).

13 John Campbell, *Geographical Memoir of Melville Island and Port Essington on the Cobourg Peninsula, Northern Australia: With Some Observations on the Settlements*

Which Have Been Established on the North Coast of New Holland (London: Royal Geographical Society, 1834), 155.

14 Barry Puruntatameri, oral history interview with authors, 9 September 2016.

15 JE Heere (ed.), *The Part Borne by the Dutch in the Discovery of Australia 1606–1765, Translated by C Stoffel* (London: Luzac, 1899), 71; John Morris, *The Tiwi: From Isolation to Cultural Change: A History of Encounters Between an Island People and Outside Forces* (Darwin: Northern Territory University Press, 2001), 31.

16 Richard Henry Major, *Early Voyages to Terra Australis, Now Called Australia: A Collection of Documents, and Extracts from Early Manuscript Maps, Illustrative of the History of Discovery on the Coasts of That Vast Island, from the Beginning of the Sixteenth Century to the Time of Captain Cook*, (London: Hakluyt Society, 1859), 168–169; Barry Puruntatameri, oral history interview with authors, 9 September 2016.

17 Barry Puruntatameri, oral history interview with authors, 9 September 2016.

18 Bede Tungutalum, oral history interview with authors, 31 August 2016.

19 Richard Tungutalum, oral history interview with authors, 2 September 2016.

20 Barry Puruntatameri, oral history interview with authors, 9 September 2016.

21 Richard Tungutalum, oral history interview with Laura Rademaker, 2 September 2016.

22 Letter from John Barrow to Under Secretary Horton, 30 April 1825, in Frederick Watson (ed.), *Historical Records of Australia* (Sydney: Government Printer, 1922) Series 3, Vol. 5, 793.

23 Campbell, *Geographical Memoir*, 150.

24 Phillip P King, *Narrative of a Survey of the Intertropical and Western Coasts of Australia: Performed Between the Years 1818 and 1822* (London: John Murray, 1826).

25 Thomas Braidwood Wilson, *Narrative of a Voyage Round the World: Comprehending an Account of the Wreck of the Ship 'Governor Ready' in Torres Straits; a Description of the British Settlements on the Coasts of New Holland, More Particularly Raffles Bay, Melville Island, Swan River, and King George's Sound; Also to Manners and Customs of the Aboriginal Tribes* (London: Sherwood, Gilbert & Piper, 1835), 123.

26 Clayton Fredericksen, 'Confinement by Isolation: Convict Mechanics and Labour at Fort Dundas, Melville Island', *Australasian Historical Archaeology*, Vol. 19 (2001), 49.

27 John Morris, 'The Tiwi and the British: An Ill-Fated Outpost', *Aboriginal History*, Vol. 25 (2001), 245.

28 Fredericksen, 'Confinement by Isolation', 50; Derek Pugh, *The British in North Australia: Fort Dundas 1824–29* (Rapid Creek: Derek Pugh, 2017), 69.

29 Morris, 'The Tiwi and the British', 246.

30 Gordon Bremer, 'Form of Taking Possession of Melville and Bathurst Islands', 1824, in Frederick Watson (ed.), *Historical Records of Australia* (Sydney: Government Printer, 1922) Series 3, Vol. 5, 781.

31 King, *Narrative of a Survey*.

32 Pye, *The Tiwi Islands*, 12.

33 Pugh, *The British in North Australia*, 117.

34 Letter(s) from Gordon Bremer to JW Croker, 11 November 1824 in Frederick Watson (ed.), *Historical Records of Australia* (Sydney: Government Printer, 1922) Series 3, Vol. 5, 772.

35 Bremer to JW Croker, 11 November 1824.

36 Richard Tungutalum, oral history interview with authors, 2 September 2016.
37 James Darren Puantulura, oral history interview with authors, 24 March 2022.
38 Richard Tungutalum, oral history interview with authors, 2 September 2016.
39 Richard Tungutalum, oral history interview with authors, 2 September 2016.
40 Bede Tungutalum, oral history interview with authors, 31 August 2016.
41 Bremer to JW Croker, 11 November 1824.
42 Bremer to JW Croker, 11 November 1824; Henry Ennis, *Remarks on Board His Majesty's Ship Tamar: In a Voyage from England to Port Praia, Cape of Good Hope, New South Wales, and from Thence Along the Coast of Australia, to Port Essington in the Cobourg Peninsula, and Thence to Bathurst and Melville Islands, Apsley's Straits, Between 27th February & the 13th of November 1824; and Continued in the Ship Countess of Harcourt, to the Isle of France, to 7th February 1825* (South Melbourne, Victoria; Richard Griffin Publisher Pty Ltd, 1983), 15.
43 Bremer to JW Croker, 11 November 1824.
44 Morris, 'The Tiwi and the British', 253; John Campbell, *Geographical Memoir*, 152.
45 Campbell, *Geographical Memoir*, 154–155.
46 Eric Venbrux, *A Death in the Tiwi Islands: Conflict, Ritual and Social Life in an Australian Aboriginal Community* (Cambridge: Cambridge University Press, 1995), 16–19.
47 James Darren Puantulura, oral history interview with authors, 24 March 2022.
48 James Darren Puantulura, oral history interview with authors, 24 March 2022.
49 Campbell, *Geographical Memoir*, 156.
50 James Darren Puantulura, oral history with authors, 24 March 2022.
51 Campbell, *Geographical Memoir*, 158.
52 Barry Puruntatameri, oral history interview with authors, 9 September 2016.
53 Morris, 'The Tiwi and the British', 254.
54 Barry Puruntatameri, oral history interview with authors, 9 September 2016.
55 James Darren Puantulura, oral history interview with authors, 24 March 2022.
56 Fredericksen, 'Confinement by Isolation', 51.
57 Letter from John Campbell to Colonial Secretary Macleay, Melville Island, 8 April 1872, Frederick Watson (ed.), *Historical Records of Australia* (Sydney: Government Printer, 1922) Series 3, Vol. 5, 800; Letter from John Campbell to Colonial Secretary Macleay, Melville Island, 8 April 1872, Frederick Watson (ed.), *Historical Records of Australia* (Sydney: Government Printer, 1922) Series 3, Vol. 5, 807.
58 Fredericksen, 'Confinement by Isolation', 52.
59 Letter from John Campbell to Colonial Secretary Macleay, Melville Island, 8 April 1872, Frederick Watson (ed.), *Historical Records of Australia* (Sydney: Government Printer, 1922) Series 3, Vol. 5, 808.
60 Campbell, *Geographical Memoir*, 154.
61 Wilson, *Narrative of a Voyage Round the World*, 125; Venbrux, *A Death in the Tiwi Islands*, 39.
62 Campbell, *Geographical Memoir*, 154.
63 Wilson, *Narrative of a Voyage Round the World*, 125.
64 Morris, 'The Tiwi and the British', 256; Fredericksen, 'Confinement by Isolation', 49.
65 Campbell, *Geographical Memoir*, 124.
66 Bede Tungutalum, oral history interview with authors, 31 August 2016.
67 Venbrux, *A Death in the Tiwi Islands*, 39.

68 John Morris, 'Memories of the Buffalo Shooters: Joe Cooper and the Tiwi (1895–1936)', *Aboriginal History*, Vol. 24 (2000), 141.
69 Bernard Tipiloura, oral history interview with authors, 20 June 2016.
70 Romolo Kantilla, oral history interview with authors, 22 November 2015.
71 Morris, 'Memories of the Buffalo Shooters', 143–144.
72 Paddy Porkilari, oral history interview with John Morris, 16 February 1965, cited in Morris, 'Memories of the Buffalo Shooters', 142.
73 WG Stretton, 'Death of Harriet a Native Woman', *R. J. Cooper – of Melville Is. Charges made against*, A3, NT1916/245, National Archives of Australia.
74 Morris, 'Memories of the Buffalo Shooters', 144; Venbrux, *A Death in the Tiwi Islands*, 40; HJM Venbrux, 'Indigenous Religion in an Intercultural Space', L Zimmer-Tamakoshi and J Dickerson-Putman (eds.), *Pulling the Right Threads: The Ethnographic Life and Legacy of Jane C Goodale*, (Urbana and Chicago: University of Illinois Press, 2008), 171–173.
75 Neville Wommatakimmi, oral history interview with authors, 26 March 2022.
76 Sam Green, n.d.; Letter from Sam Green to Minister of External Affairs, 7 September 1915, *RJ Cooper – of Melville Is. Charges Made Against*, A3, NT1916/245, National Archives of Australia; WG Stretton, 'Death of Harriet a Native Woman', *RJ Cooper – of Melville Is. Charges Made Against*, A3, NT1916/245, National Archives of Australia.
77 Barry Puruntatameri, oral history interview with authors, 9 September 2016.
78 Richard Tungutalum, oral history interview with authors, 2 September 2016.

5   Come and meet this fella

1 Iwaidja Country is on the Cobourg Peninsula on the Northern Territory mainland, northeast of Darwin. It is the closest neighbouring Country to the Tiwi.

6   Come and see

1 Romolo Kantilla, oral history interview with authors, 22 November 2015.
2 Oral history interview with authors, 23 September 2015; Jacinta Tipungwuti, personal communication with Laura Rademaker, 28 May 2019. Some Tiwi historians preferred to remain anonymous so their names are omitted.
3 Teddy Portaminni, oral history interview with authors, 26 March 2022.
4 Eugene Stockton, 'Maverick Missionaries: An Overlooked Chapter in the History of Catholic Missions', Tony Swain and Deborah Bird Rose (eds.), *Aboriginal Australians and Christian Missions: Ethnographic and Historical Studies* (Adelaide: Australian Association for the Study of Religions, 1988), 202.
5 Stefano Girola, 'Rhetoric and Action: The Policies and Attitudes of the Catholic Church with Regard to Australia's Indigenous Peoples, 1885–1967', PhD Thesis, University of Queensland, (2006), 50.
6 Girola, 'Rhetoric and Action', 32.
7 'On the Propagation of The Faith Among the Aborigines', *New Zealand Tablet*, 28 December 1888.
8 Girola, 'Rhetoric and Action', 33, 44, 63, 72; 'St Mary's Cathedral', *The Sydney Morning Herald*, 30 January, 1888, 6.
9 Oral history interview with authors, 23 September 2015.
10 Neville Wommatakimmi, oral history interview with authors, 26 March 2022.
11 Letter from FX Gsell to 'Réverend Père', 6 August 1907, Box 0700, MSC Archives Kensington.

12   Gsell, 'My Fifty Years of mission Life'.

13   Gsell, 'My Fifty Years of mission Life'.

14   'Blessing of the Training College of the Missionaries of the Sacred Heart at Kensington', *Australian Annals*, 1 January 1898, 34.

15   Caruana, *Monastery on the Hill*, 335.

16   'Northern Territory ma grande et belle province appellée Kimberley … Cette province est très riche mais encore peu peuplée de blancs, les noirs par contre y sont très nombreux … Les Pères Catholiques y ont une mission à Beagle Bay, mais à part la petite paroisse de Broome au sud de Beagle B. il[s] ne s'occupent que des noirs et encore que des noirs qui sont dans le voisinage de leur monastère.' Letter from FX Gsell to 'Réverend Père', Box 0700, MSC Archives Kensington, translated by Alexis Bergantz.

17   'Si je les obtiens nous aurons là un champ de mission idéale. Les sauvages sans doute n'y sont pas tellement nombreux; mais une fois la mission organisée, on pourra facilement induire les natifs de la terre ferme de venir s'y établir, et ainsi sous la protection et avec l'aide du Gouvernement on pourra organiser un espèce de [réservation] ou Etat indigène tout à fait séparé des blancs et se subvenant à lui-même.' Letter from FX Gsell to 'Réverend Père', 5 June 1909, Box 0700, MSC Archives Kensington.

18   Gsell, 'My Fifty Years of Mission Life'.

19   Letter from FX Gsell to SJ Mitchell, 25 July 1910, in 'Bathurst Island – Reserve for Aborigines', A1, 1938/33126, National Archives of Australia.

20   Teddy Portaminni, oral history interview with authors, 26 March 2022.

21   Genevieve Campbell, 'Ngarukuruwala – We Sing: The Songs of the Tiwi Islands, Northern Australia', PhD Thesis, University of Sydney (2013), 431.

22   Gsell, 'My Fifty Years of Mission Life'.

23   Personal communication with authors, 9 June 2016.

24   Charles William Merton Hart, 'The sons of Turimpi', American Anthropologist, Vol. 56, No. 2 (1954), 244–251.

25   'Land Ownership', Tiwi Land Council website, <tiwilandcouncil.com/index. cfm?fuseaction=page&p=228&l=2&id=60&smid=116>.

26   Eric Venbrux, *A Death in the Tiwi Islands: Conflict, Ritual, and Social Life in an Australian Aboriginal Community* (Cambridge: Cambridge University Press, 1995), 24.

27   Personal communication with authors, 9 June 2016.

28   Sam Green, 10 November 1914, A3, NT1916/245, National Archives of Australia.

29   Gsell, 'My Fifty Years of Mission Life'.

30   Francis Xavier Gsell, *'The Bishop with 150 Wives': Fifty Years as a Missionary* (Sydney: Angus and Robertson, 1955), 47–48.

31   Oral history interview with authors, 23 September 2015.

32   Francesca Merlan, *Dynamics of Difference in Australia: Indigenous Past and Present in a Settler Country* (Philadelphia, Pennsylvania: University of Pennsylvania Press, 2018), 30–35.

33   Personal communication with authors, 9 June 2016.

34   Dulcie Kelantumama, oral history interview with authors, 9 June 2016.

35   Romolo Kantilla, oral history interview with authors, 22 November 2015.

36   Oral history interview with authors, 28 September 2015.

37   Oral history interview with authors, 23 September 2015.

38   Teddy Portaminni, oral history interview with authors, 26 March 2022.

39   Jacinta Tipungwuti, personal communication with Laura Rademaker, 28 May 2019.

40   Merlan, *Dynamics of Difference in Australia*, 75.

41   Jean Comaroff, 'Missionaries and Mechanical Clocks: An Essay on Religion and History in South Africa', *The Journal of Religion*, Vol. 71, No. 1 (1991), 9.

42   Oral history interview with authors, 28 September 2015.

43   Bernard Tipiloura, oral history interview with authors, 20 June 2016.

44   Barry Puruntatameri, oral history interview with authors, 9 September 2016.

45   Teddy Portaminni, oral history interview with authors, 26 March 2022.

46   Gsell, *The Bishop with 150 Wives*, 50–51.

47   Oral history interview with authors, 23 September 2015.

48   FX Gsell, 'Reseignments' (1913), Box 0564, MSC Archives Kensington.

49   John Pye, 'Bathurst Island or Nguiu 1977–1976', (1978), Box 0564, MSC Archives Kensington.

50   Alana Harris, *Faith in the Family: A Lived Religious History of English Catholicism, 1945–1982* (Oxford: Oxford University Press, 2016), 207.

51   St Therese of Lisieux, *Story of a Soul: The Autobiography of St. Therese of Lisieux: Third Edition Translated from the Original Manuscripts* (Washington, D.C.: Institute of Carmelite Studies Publications, 2013), 1–2.

52   Gsell 'My Fifty Years of Mission Life'; Gsell, *'The Bishop with 150 Wives'*, 35.

53   Gsell, 'My Fifty Years of Mission Life'.

54   Gsell, 'My Fifty Years of Mission Life'; Romolo Kantilla, oral history interview with authors, 22 November, 2015.

55   Gsell, 'My Fifty Years of Mission Life'; Gsell, *The Bishop with 150 Wives*, 73.

56   Henry Fry, 'A Bathurst Island Mourning Rite,' *Mankind*, Vol. 4, No. 2 (1949), 80.

57   HJM Venbrux, 'Indigenous Religion in an Intercultural Space', L Zimmer-Tamakoshi and J Dickerson-Putman (eds.), *Pulling the Right Threads: The Ethnographic Life and Legacy of Jane C Goodale,* (Urbana and Chicago: University of Illinois Press, 2008), 172.

58   J Holmes, 10 November 1914, A3, NT1916/245, National Archives of Australia.

59   Stanford T Shulman, Deborah L Shulman, and Ronald H Sims, 'The Tragic 1824 Journey of the Hawaiian King and Queen to London History of Measles in Hawaii', *Pediatric Infectious Disease Journal*, Vol. 28, No. 8 (2009); G Dennis Shanks et al., 'Extreme Mortality After First Introduction of Measles Virus to the Polynesian Island of Rotuma, 1911', *American Journal of Epidemiology*, Vol. 173, Issue. 10 (2011), 1211.

60   Henry Fry, 'A Bathurst Island Mourning Rite', 80.

61   Venbrux, 'Indigenous Religion', 176, 183.

62   Jane Goodale, *Tiwi Wives: A Study of the Women of Melville Island, North Australia* (Seattle: University of Washington Press, 1971), 224.

63   Venbrux, 'Indigenous Religion', 170.

64   Richard Tungutalum, oral history interview with authors, 2 September 2016.

65   Barry Puruntatameri, oral history interview with authors, 9 September 2016.

66   Letter from Administrator to Secretary of Department of External Affairs, 9 June 1916, A3, NT1916/2359, National Archives of Australia; Gilruth, 21 December 1915, A3, NT1916/245, National Archives of Australia; Gsell, *The Bishop with 150 Wives*, 49; Jane Goodale, *Melville Island Expedition 1954 Field Notebook*, Series 1, Item 2, MS4676 Jane Goodale Papers, AIATSIS.

8   The girl who turned her world around

1   John Morris, 'Continuing "Assimilation"?: A Shifting Identity for the Tiwi 1919 to the Present', PhD Thesis, University of Ballarat, (2003), 64; John Morris, 'Life History of a Tiwi Man', MSC Archives, Box 0564.

2   Alf Dyer, 'Oenpelli Report December 1928', Northern Territory Archives Service NTRS 1099/P1.

3   'Aboriginal Memos' 194[?], MSS 6040/7, Box 2, Mitchell Library, State Library of New South Wales; Ted Egan, 'Suggested form to be signed by relation of single boy', 1958, F1, 1957/1795, National Archives of Australia.

4   JRB Love, *The Aborigines: Their Present Condition as Seen in Northern South Australia, the Northern Territory, North-West Australia and Western Queensland* (Melbourne: Board of Missions of the Prebysterian Church of Australia, 1915), 49.

5   Regina Ganter, 'Bathurst Island Mission', *German Missionaries in Australia*, Griffith University (2009–2018). Available online: < missionaries.griffith.edu.au/>.

6   'A trip with the Blacks of Bathurst Island', *Australian Annals*, 1 January 1918, 24.

7   'The Northern Territory', *The Catholic Press*, 14 November 1918.

8   Oral history interview with authors, 26 September 2015.

9   Oral history interview with authors, 23 September 2015.

10   Jane Goodale, '"Taramaguti" Today: Changing Roles of Senior Tiwi Wives as Household Managers', *Pacific Studies*, Vol. 19, No. 4. (1996), 134163.

11   Goodale, '"Taramaguti" Today', 135–136.

12   Personal communication with Laura Rademaker, 9 June 2016.

13   Goodale, '"Taramaguti" Today', 137; Jane Goodale, *Tiwi Wives: A Study of the Women of Melville Island, North Australia* (Seattle: University of Washington Press, 1971), 228.

14   Oral history interview with authors, 23 September 2015.

15   Francillia Puruntatameri, oral history interview with authors, 23 March 2022.

16   Goodale, '"Taramaguti" Today', 137; Jane Goodale, *Tiwi Wives*, 46.

17   Oral history interview with authors, 26 September 2015.

18   Oral history interview with authors, 26 September 2015.

19   Goodale, '"Taramaguti" Today', 138.

20   Oral history interview with authors, 26 September 2015.

21   Francillia Puruntatameri, oral history interview with authors, 23 March 2022.

22   Oral history interview with authors, 26 September 2015.

23   Francillia Puruntatameri, oral history interview with authors, 23 March 2022.

24   Oral history interview with authors, 26 September 2015.

25   Oral history interview with authors, 28 September 2015.

26   Oral history interview with authors, 23 November 2015.

27   Goodale, Tiwi Wives, 51, 132–134; Jane Goodale, 'Social organisation – local organisation. Notes on marriage and "countries".', n.d., Series 11, Item 10, MS 4676 Jane C Goodale papers, Australian Institute of Aboriginal and Torres Strait Islander Studies.

28   Gsell, *The Bishop with 150 Wives*, 88; Goodale, *Tiwi Wives*, 126.

29   FX Gsell, 'Report about Bathurst Island Mission', nd, in 'Bathurst Island Mission Reports – Northern Territory', A431, 1951/1294, National Archives of Australia.

30   Eric Venbrux, *A Death in the Tiwi Islands: Conflict, Ritual, and Social Life in an Australian Aboriginal Community* (Cambridge: Cambridge University Press, 1995), 29, 41, 227.

31 Children's education has often been used as an incentive for Indigenous people to allow missionaries to baptise their children, both in Tiwi and other Indigenous communities.

32 John O'Carrigan & John Morris, 'Christian Marriage and Family Life on Bathurst Island', *Arnhem Land Epistle,* October 1964; see also Jane Collier, *Marriage and Inequality in Classless Societies* (Stanford, California: Stanford University Press, 1993), 35.

33 John Fallon, 'The Good Old Days', *Nelen Yubu,* vol. 48 (1991), 14; Venbrux, *A Death in the Tiwi Islands,* 227.

34 Oral history interview with authors, 26 September 2015.

35 Richard Tungutalum, oral history interview with Laura Rademaker, 2 September 2016.

36 Oral history interview with authors, 26 September 2015.

37 Mavis Kerinaiua, oral history interview with Laura Rademaker, 19 June 2016.

38 Oral history interview with authors, 23 November 2015.

39 Oral history interview with authors, 26 September 2015.

40 Oral history interview with authors, 25 September 2015.

41 Oral history interview with authors, 28 September 2015.

42 Susan Sleeper-Smith, 'Women, Kin, and Catholicism: New perspectives on the fur trade', *Ethnohistory,* Vol. 47, No. 2 (2000), 425–427.

43 Oral history interview with authors, 23 November 2015.

44 Tiffany Shellam, *Shaking Hands on the Fringe: Negotiating the Aboriginal World at King George's Sound* (Crawley: UWA Press, 2009), 188–190; Sophie White, *Wild Frenchmen and Frenchified Indians: Material Culture and Race in Colonial Louisiana* (Philadelphia, Pennsylvania: University of Pennsylvania Press, 2013), 76.

45 Eric Venbrux, *A Death in the Tiwi Islands: Conflict, Ritual, and Social Life in an Australian Aboriginal Community* (Cambridge: Cambridge University Press, 1995), 18, 55; Jane Goodale, *Melville Island Expedition 1954 Field Notebook,* Series 1, Item 2, MS4676 Jane Goodale Papers, Australian Institute of Aboriginal and Torres Strait Islander Studies.

46 Oral history interview with authors, 26 September 2015.

47 Sue Crawford, 'Spears to Crosses: An Anthropological Analysis of the Social Systems of Missionaries in Northern Australia', Honours Thesis, Australian National University (1978), 23.

48 Elaine Tiparui, oral history interview with Laura Rademaker, 31 August 2016.

49 Marie Cecile Tipiloura, oral history interview with Laura Rademaker, 8 June 2016.

50 Oral history interview with authors, 23 November 2015.

51 Romolo Kantilla, oral history interview with Laura Rademaker, 22 November 2015.

52 Tim Rowse, *White Flour, White Power: From Rations to Citizenship in Central Australia* (Cambridge: Cambridge University Press, 1998), 207.

53 Maria Brandl, 'Pukumani: The Social Context of Bereavement in a North Australian Aboriginal Tribe', PhD Thesis, University of Western Australia (1971), 129–132, 156.

54 Morris, 'Continuing "Assimilation"?', 170; see also Venbrux, *A Death in the Tiwi Islands,* 23.

55 Romolo Kantilla, oral history interview with authors, 22 November 2015.

56 Gsell, *The Bishop with 150 Wives,* 93.

57 Henry Fry, 'A Bathurst Island Mourning Rite', *Mankind,* Vol. 4, No. 2 (1949), 179.

58   Letter from Paddy Cahill to Baldwin Spencer, 11 March 1915, Box 4a, Item 11, *Papers of Sir Baldwin Spencer*, Pitt River Museum.
59   'Garr Matthew: SERN 428: POB Thursday Island: POE at Sea HMAT A 64 Demostheues: NOK W Garr Fanny' (1914-1920), B2455, GARR M, National Archives of Australia.
60   'Report by TJ Beckett on visit made to Anson Bay District Melville Bathurst and Indian Island re Aborigines', (1916), A3, NT1916/2359, National Archives of Australia.
61   'Report by TJ Beckett', (1916), A3, NT1916/2359, National Archives of Australia.
62   'Report by TJ Beckett', (1916), A3, NT1916/2359, National Archives of Australia.
63   'Report by TJ Beckett', (1916), A3, NT1916/2359, National Archives of Australia.
64   Charles William Merton Hart, 'The sons of Turimpi', *American Anthropologist*, Vol. 56, No. 2 (1954), 251–253.
65   'Report by TJ Beckett', (1916), A3, NT1916/2359, National Archives of Australia.
66   'Garr Matthew: SERN 428: POB Thursday Island: POE At Sea HMAT A 64 Demostheues: NOK W Garr Fanny' (1914–1920), B2455, GARR M, National Archives of Australia.
67   Letter to 'Mother', 25 March 1919, MSC Archives Kensington, Box 0564.
68   John McGrath to Provincial, 3 October 1927, MSC Archives Kensington, Box 0564.

9   *Purraputumali, nginya amini* (Louie, my grandfather)

1   These are mysterious and sometimes frightening lights seen across Australia.
2   The Black Watch was an Aboriginal reconnaissance group that patrolled the region.

10   Unlikely allies.

1   Bede Tungutalum, oral history interview with authors, 31 August 2016.
2   Pye, 'Wings over the Islands', *Annals of Our Lady of the Sacred Heart*, 1 August 1945.
3   Magdalen Kelantumama, oral history with authors, 28 March 2022.
4   Magdalen Kelantumama, oral history with authors, 28 March 2022.
5   James Darren Puantulura, oral history with authors, 24 March 2022.
6   John Morris, 'Potential Allies of the Enemy: The Tiwi in World War Two', *Journal of Northern Territory History*, No. 15 (2004), 80.
7   Oral history interview with authors, 23 September 2015.
8   Magdalen Kelantumama, oral history with authors, 28 March 2022.
9   Elaine Tiparui, oral history interview with authors, 31 August 2016.
10   Francis Xavier Gsell to Propaganda Fide, 1929, MSC Kensington Archives 0564 (translation by Alexis Bergantz).
11   Gsell to Propaganda Fide, 1929, MSC Kensington 0564.
12   Regina Ganter, '"Australia Seemed Closer than Tokyo": Japanese Labourers in Australia, 1870s to 1940s', D Grant and G Seal (eds.), *Australia in the World: Perceptions and Possibilities: Papers from the Outside Images of Australia Conference, Perth, 1992* (Perth, Western Australia: Black Swan Press, 1994), 330–337.
13   Ganter, '"Australia Seemed Closer than Tokyo"'.
14   Reuben Cooper as cited in Ronald R Pryor, 1 March 1938, National Archives of Australia (hereafter NAA) F1 1938/584.
15   Murabuda Wurramarba, oral history with Laura Rademaker, 10 December 2012.

16 Charles Theodore Graham Haultain, *Watch Off Arnhem Land* (Canberra: Roebuck Society, 1971), 26.

17 Francis Gsell, 'Bathurst Island Mission Station Annual Report, 1928', NAA A431 1951/1294.

18 Francis Gsell, 'Annual Report of Bathurst Island Mission Station, January 1931' NAA A431 1951/1294.

19 'The Northern Territory. Sacred Heart Missions', *The Catholic Press*, 14 November 1918.

20 'Story of Outback Missions; Evangelists of Many Nations', *The Advertiser*, 30 June 1934.

21 'Rejoice! Rejoice!', *The Catholic Press*, 29 March 1934.

22 'Bought Native Girls Saved from Life Degradation Missioner at Bathurst Island', *Kalgoorlie Miner*, 7 April 1934.

23 'Priest Buys Native Girls to Save Them from Cruelty', *Advocate*, 29 March 1934.

24 'Interference with Natives Missionaries', *Transcontinental*, 26 October 1934.

25 'Missionary Buys 124 Girls to Save Them from Slavery', *Sunday Examiner*, 5 August 1934; *Northern Standard*, 28 September 1934.

26 'Missionary Buys 124 Girls to Save Them from Slavery'.

27 'Why Native Girls Are Bought; Tribal Laws Overcome', *The Mail*, 29 September 1934.

28 'Owner of 121 "Wives". Monsignor Gsell in Sydney', the *Sydney Morning Herald*, 18 September 1937.

29 'Abo. Girls Bartered to Japanese Swarmed Luggers like Mosquitoes', the *Courier-Mail*, 25 September 1936.

30 Gsell, 5 August 1936, MSC Kensington Box 0571.

31 Gsell to Fr Filbry, 1 April 1939, MSC Kensington Box 0571.

32 Gsell, 5 August 1936, MSC Kensington Box 0571.

33 'Tribal communions among the Aborigines. Need for Christianity', *Cairns Post*, 10 December 1937.

34 CE Cook, 16 December 1936, NAA F1 1937/600.

35 Gsell, 'Bathurst Island Mission Station Annual Report, 1928', NAA A431 1951/1294.

36 MSC Kensington, Bathurst Island, 9.

37 'Natives Barter Lubras for Food and Tobacco Amazing Revelations of Exploitation DARWIN, September 24', *Morning Bulletin*, 25 September 1936.

38 John Morris, 'The Japanese and the Aborigines: An Overview of the Efforts to Stop the Prostitution of Coastal and Island Women', *Journal of Northern Territory History*, No. 21 (2010), 24.

39 Morris, 'The Japanese and the Aborigines', 27.

40 'Britannia Rules the Waves', *Northern Standard*, 9 April 1937.

41 'Larrakia's Haul of 11 Luggers', *Courier-Mail*, 29 June 1938.

42 'Foreigners Barred from Northern Waters', *Advertiser*, 21 April 1937.

43 Gsell, Report from Diocese of Darwin to *Propaganda*, 17 August 1939, MSC 0700.

44 Elaine Tiparui, oral history interview with authors, 31 August 2016.

45 Oral history interview with authors, 23 September 2015.

46 Oral history interview with authors, 17 November 2015.

47 Bede Tungutalum, oral history interview with authors, 31 August 2016.

48 Bede Tungutalum, oral history interview with authors, 31 August 2016.

49 Oral history interview with authors, 11 June 2016.

50 Donald Thomson, 7 September 1937, NAA F1 1937/600.

51 W Cochrane, 'Press Report on Lubra Traffic in NT', 3 March 1938, NAA F1 1938/584.

52 Haultain to CLA Abbott, 3 March 1938, NAA F1 1938/584.

53 Haultain to CLA Abbott, 3 March 1938, NAA F1 1938/584.

54 Memorandum, 5 November 1922, NAA A1 1922/19013.

55 JA Carrodus, 18 September 1939, NAA A461 D349/3/4.

56 TJ Collins, 27 February 1941, NAA A461 D349/3/4.

57 Philip Collier, 7 May 1936, NAA A461 D349/3/4.

58 Philip Collier, 29 April 1936, NAA A461 D349/3/4.

59 HS Foll to SH Davies, nd NAA A461 D349/3/4.

60 Philip Collier, 29 April 1936, NAA A461 D349/3/4.

61 Gsell, nd NAA F1 1938/584.

62 WHV Waterson, 9 December 1938, NAA A432 1938/502 Pearling Ordinance 1930–1937.

63 Haultain, *Watch Off Arnhem Land*, 41.

64 'Myall' is an offensive term that referred to Aboriginal people who lived in the bush.

65 NAA F1 1938/584.

66 'Raid on Pearling Luggers: Aboriginal Women Found Aboard: Capture by Larrakia', *Northern Standard*, 7 March 1939.

67 'Luggers and Lubras: Case Before Court', *Northern Standard*, 7 September 1939.

68 K Nylander, 15 March 1939, NAA A659 1939/1/8519.

69 Bernard Tipiloura, oral history interview with authors, 20 June 2016.

70 Magdalen Kelantumama, oral history with authors, 28 March 2022.

71 Henrietta Hunter, oral history with authors, 19 November 2015.

72 Pye, 'Wings over the Islands', *Annals of Our Lady of the Sacred Heart*, 1 August 1945.

73 Bede Tungutalum, oral history interview with authors, 31 August 2016.

74 Some Tiwi refer to Macassans and Japanese interchangeably.

75 Oral history interview with authors, 28 September 2015.

76 Elaine Tiparui, oral history interview with authors, 31 August 2016.

77 Oral history interview with authors, 26 September 2015.

78 Walter Kerinaiua, oral history with authors, 24 March 2022.

79 Oral history interview with authors, 11 June 2016.

80 Pirrawayingi, oral history with authors, 5 September 2016.

81 Bede Tungutalum, oral history interview with authors, 31 August 2016.

82 Munkara, Marie, *Every Secret Thing*, University of Queensland Press, 2009; Munkara, Marie, *Of Ashes and Rivers That Run to the Sea*, Random House Australia, 2016.

83 Robert A Hall, *The Black Diggers* (Canberra: Aboriginal Studies Press, 1997), 131.

84 'Darwin Raid to-morrow – Japanese Boast', *The Age*, 26 Feb 1942, 3.

85 Noah Riseman, 'Contesting White Knowledge: Yolngu Stories from World War II', *The Oral History Review*, Vol 37, Issue 2 (2010), 175.

86 Noah Riseman, *Defending Whose Country?: Indigenous Soldiers in the Pacific War* (Lincoln, Nebraska: University of Nebraska Press, 2012), 81. Geoffrey Gray, 'The Army Requires Anthropologists: Australian Anthropologists at War, 1939–1946', *Australian Historical Studies*, Vol. 37, No. 127, (2006), 168.

87 Australian Water Transport Operating Company Diary, September–December 1943, Royal Australian Artillery, AWM52 5/45/6/1, Unit War Diaries, 1939–45 War, Australian War Memorial, digitised collection.

88 Australian Water Transport Operating Company Diary, September–December 1943, Royal Australian Artillery.

89 Hall, *The Black Diggers*, 101.

90 Magdalen Kelantumama, oral history with authors, 28 March 2022.

91 Pye, 'Bathurst Island War Effort', *Annals of Our Lady of the Sacred Heart*, 1 March 1946, 69; Pye, 'Wings over the Islands', *Annals of Our Lady of the Sacred Heart*, 1 August 1945.

92 Karen Tipiloura, oral history with authors, 23 March 2022.

93 James Darren Puantulura, oral history with authors, 24 March 2022.

94 Frances Kerinaiua, oral history with authors, 11 June 2016.

95 Karen Tipiloura, oral history with authors, 23 March 2022.

96 *Tiwi Heroes: World War Two Encounters*, NT Library exhibition, March 2022.

97 Pye, 'Bathurst Island War Effort', *Annals of Our Lady of the Sacred Heart*, 1 March 1946, 71.

98 Pye, 'Bathurst Island War Effort', *Annals of Our Lady of the Sacred Heart*, 1 March 1946, 70–71.

99 Magdalen Kelantumama, oral history with authors, 28 March 2022.

100 Harry Munkara, 1973. NAA F1 T65 1972/8313.

101 Magdalen Kelantumama, oral history with authors, 28 March 2022.

102 Harry Munkara, 1973. NAA F1 T65 1972/8313.

103 Hall, *The Black Diggers*, 101; John Morris, 'Continuing "Assimilation"?: A Shifting Identity for the Tiwi, 1919 to the Present', PhD thesis, Federation University (2003), 155.

104 Pirrawayingi, oral history with authors, 5 September 2016.

105 J O'Carrigan to HC Giese, 13 January, 194[?] NAA F941 1970/435.

106 HG Giese to CC Allom, 27 September 1963.

107 HC Giese to CC Allom, 13 May 1964, NAA F941 1970/435.

108 TC Lovegrove to Evans, 8 November 1973, NAA F1 T65 1972/8313.

109 *Tiwi Heroes: World War Two Encounters*, NT Library exhibition, March 2022.

12 Creating a sanctuary

1 *Assimilation for our Aborigines* (Canberra: Govt. Printer, 1958).

2 Henschke to Provincial, 11 December 1934, Box 0564, MSC Archives Kensington.

3 Francis X Gsell to Father Filbry 24 December 1934, Box 0571, MSC Archives Kensington.

4 Calista Kantilla, oral history interview with authors, 23 March 2022.

5 Oral history interview with authors, 6 September 2016; oral history interview with authors, 23 September 2015; oral history interview with authors, 30 August 2016.

6 Oral history interview with authors, 30 August 2016.

7 Elaine Tiparui, oral history interview with authors, 31 August 2016.

8 Elaine Tiparui, oral history interview with authors, 31 August 2016.

9 Oral history interview with authors, 28 September 2016.

10 Elaine Tiparui, oral history interview with authors, 31 August 2016.

11 Oral history interview with authors, 30 August 2016.

12   Oral history interview with authors, 28 September 2016; Magdalen Kelantumama, oral history with authors, 28 March 2022.

13   Oral history interview with authors, 23 September 2016.

14   Bernard Tipiloura, oral history interview with authors, 20 June 2016.

15   Henschke to Provincial, 23 September 1943, in Box 0560, MSC Archives Kensington.

16   Giese to Bishop O'Loughlin, 21 August 1964, in Box 0560, MSC Archives Kensington.

17   Magdalen Kelantumama, oral history interview with authors, 28 March 2022.

18   Magdalen Kelantumama, oral history interview with authors, 28 March 2022.

19   Teresita Puruntatameri, oral history interview with authors, 23 November 2015.

20   Oral history interview with authors, 30 August 2016.

21   Marie Cecile Tipiloura oral history interview with authors, 8 June 2016.

22   Enid Cunningham, oral history interview with authors, 6 September 2016.

23   Oral history interview with the authors, 24 September 2015.

24   Frances Kerinaiua, oral history interview with authors, 11 June 2016.

25   Oral history interview with authors, 30 August 2016.

26   Elaine Tiparui, oral history interview with authors, 31 August 2016.

27   Magdalen Kelantumama, oral history interview with authors, 28 March 2022.

28   Teddy Portaminni, oral history interview with authors, 26 March 2022.

29   Elaine Tiparui, oral history interview with authors, 31 August 2016.

30   Oral history interview with authors, 6 September 2016.

31   Oral history interview with authors, 28 September 2015.

32   James Darren Puantulura, oral history interview with authors, 24 March 2022.

33   Magdalen Kelantumama, oral history interview with authors, 28 March 2022.

34   Calista Kantilla, oral history interview with authors, 1 September 2016.

35   Calista Kantilla, oral history interview with authors, 1 September 2016.

36   Oral history interview with authors, 30 August 2016.

37   Elaine Tipiloura, oral history interview with authors, 31 August 2016.

38   Calista Kantilla, oral history interview with authors, 1 September 2016.

39   Calista Kantilla, oral history interview with authors, 1 September 2016.

40   Calista Kantilla, oral history interview with authors, 1 September 2016.

41   Oral history interview with authors, 26 September 2015.

42   Oral history interview with authors, 26 September 2015.

43   Neville Wommatakimmi, oral history interview with authors, 26 March 2022.

44   Kerryann Kerinaiua, oral history interview with authors, 26 March 2022.

45   James Darren Puantulua, oral history interview with authors, 24 March 2022.

46   John Morris, 'Continuing "Assimilation"?: A Shifting Identity for the Tiwi 1919 to the Present', PhD Thesis, University of Ballarat (2003), 62.

47   Teddy Portaminni, oral history interview with authors, 26 March 2022.

48   Ted Egan and Bill Gammage, *Ted Egan Interviewed by Bill Gammage* [Sound Recording], 2003.

49   Egan and Gammage, *Ted Egan Interviewed by Bill Gammage*.

50   FH Moy, 'Review Report: Bathurst Island – Roman Catholic Mission', 9 August 1950, A431 1951/1294, NAA.

51   M Culnane, 'Bathurst Island Catholic Mission for Full Blood Aborigines – Review Report', 11 September 1951, A431 1951/1294, NAA.

52   CR Lambert, 'Review Report – Bathurst Island Full-Blood Mission', F1, 1964/65, NAA.

53 Colin Tatz, 'Aboriginal Administration in the Northern Territory of Australia', PhD Thesis, Australian National University, (1964), 50.

54 John McMahon to Kerrins 196[?], Box 0561a, MSC Archives Kensington.

55 Henschke to Provincial, 16 October 1943, Box 0560, MSC Archives Kensington.

56 Morris, 'Continuing "Assimilation"?', 223.

57 EP Milliken, 'Bathurst Island Mission – Inspection Report, May 1961' A452, 1961/5702, NAA.

58 EP Milliken, 'Bathurst Island Mission – Inspection Report, May 1961' A452, 1961/5702, NAA.

59 O'Loughlin to Provincial, 20 June 1963, Box 0560, MSC Archives Kensington.

60 CR Lambert to Administrator of the Northern Territory, 26 October 1961, A452, 1961/5702, NAA.

61 Giese to Hasluck, 28 December 1962, F1, 1964/608, NAA; 'Causes and Numbers of Infant Deaths at Bathurst Island for Period 1.1.61 to 26.2.63', F1, 1964/608, NAA.

62 Morris, 'Continuing "Assimilation"?', 225.

63 JP O'Loughlin, 'Status of Aboriginal Marriages', A452, 1961/3786, NAA.

64 Marion, 'Part to be Played by Aboriginal Women in Programme of Assimilation', 1957, NTAS 2972.

65 Marion, 'Part to be Played by Aboriginal Women in Programme of Assimilation', 1957, NTAS 2972.

66 Calista Kantilla, oral history interview with authors, 1 September 2016.

67 Calista Kantilla, oral history interview with authors, 1 September 2016.

68 Calista Kantilla, oral history interview with authors, 1 September 2016.

69 Magdalen Kelantumama, oral history interview with authors, 28 March 2022.

70 Oral history interview with authors, 23 September 2015.

71 Marie Cecile Tipiloura, oral history interview with authors, 8 June 2016.

72 Teresita Puruntatameri, oral history interview with authors, 23 November 2015.

73 Oral history interview with authors, 23 September 2015.

74 Calista Kantilla, oral history interview with Laura Rademaker, 1 September 2016.

75 Calista Kantilla, oral history interview with Laura Rademaker, 1 September 2016.

76 Oral history interview with authors, 24 September 2015.

77 Enid Cunningham, oral history interview with authors, 6 September 2016.

78 Magdalen Kelantumama, oral history with authors, 28 March 2022.

79 O'Loughlin to Kerrins, 7 February 1954, in Box 0560, MSC Archives Kensington.

80 Copas to A Breene, 3 November 1956, in Box 0560, MSC Archives Kensington.

81 O'Loughlin to … Kerrins, 15 April 1959, in Box 0560, MSC Archives Kensington.

82 Copas to A Breene, November 1956, in Box 0560, MSC Archives Kensington.

83 Father Clancy, 1966 report in Box 0560, MSC Archives Kensington.

84 Report to Provincial Council, May 1971, in Box 0561a, MSC Archives Kensington.

14 Converting the world

1 As told by Francillia Puruntatameri.

2 Oral history with authors, 28 September 2015.

3 Oral history with authors, 24 September 2015.

4 Calista Kantilla, oral history with authors, 1 September 2016.

5 Eric Venbrux, *A death in the Tiwi Islands: Conflict, ritual, and social life in an Australian Aboriginal community*, Cambridge 1995, 61.

6	Charles P Mountford, *The Tiwi: Their Art, Myth, and Ceremony*, London 1958, 61.

7	Pirrawayingi Marius Puruntatameri, personal communication with Laura Rademaker, 17 June 2016.

8	Jane Goodale, *Tiwi Wives: A Study of the Women of Melville Island, North Australia*, Washington DC 1971, 310.

9	Goodale, *Tiwi Wives*, 259.

10	Elaine Tiparui, oral history with authors, 31 August 2016.

11	'*Mauliantanili awangtini tangini mu mu*', Mountford, *The Tiwi*, 30.

12	'Mythology', Australian Institute of Aboriginal and Torres Strait Islander Studies (hereafter AIATSIS), MS 4540 CWM Hart papers.

13	Bernard Tipiloura, oral history with authors, 20 June 2016.

14	Gsell, 'Report about Bathurst Island Mission', nd, MSC 0564.

15	Fallon, 'The Good Old Days' *Nelen Yubu* 48, 1991, 13.

16	John Morris, 'Continuing "Assimilation"?: A Shifting Identity for the Tiwi 1919 to the Present' (PhD thesis, University of Ballarat, 2003), 259.

17	'Annual Report Bathurst Island Mission, 1962–1963', National Archives of Australia (Hereafter NAA) F1 1962/1051.

18	'Comparison of Bathurst Island with other Government and Mission Settlements', 25 October 1963, NAA F1 1962/1051.

19	Marie Cecile Tipiloura, oral history with authors, 8 June 2016.

20	'*Ngawenterapenamanjimi all-together kuwijelanjimi*' in Maria Brandl, 'Pukumani: The Social Context of Bereavement in a North Australian Aboriginal Tribe' (PhD thesis, University of Western Australia, 1971), 508.

21	Mountford, *The Tiwi*, 60.

22	Jane Goodale, 'Melville Island Expedition, Field Notebook', Volume 1, AIATSIS MS 4676, Series 1, Item 1.

23	Goodale, *Tiwi Wives*, 255–256.

24	Francis Kerinaiua, oral history with authors, 11 June 2016; Morris, 'Continuing "Assimilation"?', 257.

25	Morris, 'Continuing "Assimilation"?', 257.

26	Pye, 'Bathurst Island or Nguiu', MSC 0564.

27	Oral history with authors, 23 September 2015.

28	Venbrux, *Death in the Tiwi Islands*, 59, 61, 116, 216.

29	Barry Puruntatameri, oral history with authors, 23 November 2015.

30	Venbrux, *Death in the Tiwi Islands*, 59, 61, 116, 216.

31	Calista Kantilla, oral history with authors, 1 September 2016.

32	Pirrawayingi Puruntatameri, personal communication with Laura Rademaker, 17 June 2016.

33	Oral history with authors, 26 September 2015.

34	Romolo Kantilla, oral history with authors, 22 November 2015.

35	Barry Puruntatameri, oral history with authors, 23 November. 2015.

36	Oral history with authors, 23 September 2015.

37	Calista Kantilla, oral history with authors, 1 September 2016.

38	Oral history with authors, 24 September 2015.

39	Romolo Kantilla, oral history with authors, 22 November 2015.

40	Barry Puruntatameri, oral history with authors, 23 November 2015.

41	'Summary of Proceedings of Missions/Administration Conference 5th–9th June 1967', NAA A452 NT1967/4400.

42 Pirrawayingi Puruntatameri, personal communication with Laura Rademaker, 17 June 2016.

43 John W O'Malley, *What Happened at Vatican II* (Cambridge, Mass, Harvard University Press 2010), 13–14.

44 *Declaration on the Relation of the Church to Non-Christian Religions*, Nostra Aetate, proclaimed by Pope Paul VI, 28 October 1965.

45 'Minutes of Meeting Called by Bishop JP O'Loughlin MSC', July 1968, MSC 0561a.

46 Michael Sims, 'Liturgy among the Aborigines', nd, MSC 0562a.

47 John Morris, 'Christianity Welcomes Tribal Lore', Arnhem Land Epistle (December 1968), 1.

48 Patrick Dodson, Jacinta Elston, and Brian McCoy, 'Leaving Culture at the Door: Aboriginal Perspectives on Christian Belief and Practice', *Pacifica: Australasian Theological Studies* 19, No. 3 (2006), 256.

49 Oral history with authors, 23 September 2015.

50 Address of John Paul II to the Aborigines and Torres Strait Islanders in Blatherskite Park, Alice Springs, 29 November 1986, available online: <w2. vatican.va/content/john-paul-ii/en/speeches/1986/november/documents/hf_jp-ii_spe_19861129_aborigeni-alice-springs-australia.html>

51 Dominic O'Sullivan, *Faith, Politics and Reconciliation: Catholicism and the Politics of Indigeneity* (ATF Press, 2005), 123.

52 O'Sullivan, 123.

53 Laura Rademaker and Tim Rowse, 'How Shall We Write the History of Self-Determination in Australia?', *Indigenous Self-Determination in Australia: Histories and Historiography*, 2020, 1–36.

54 Laura Rademaker, 'An Emerging Protestant Doctrine of Self-Determination in the Northern Territory', *Self-Determination in Australia*, 2020, 59.

55 John Morris, 'Continuing "Assimilation"?: A Shifting Identity for the Tiwi 1919 to the Present' (PhD Thesis, University of Ballarat, 2003), 286–287.

56 Richard Tungutalum, oral history with authors, 2 September 2016.

57 *Catholic Weekly*, 29 June 1961, cited in Arnold R Pilling, 'A Historical versus a Non-Historical Approach to Social Change and Continuity among the Tiwi', *Oceania* 32, No. 4 (1962), 324.

58 Colin Tatz, 'Aboriginal Administration in the Northern Territory of Australia' (Australian National University, 1964), 207.

59 Morris, 'Continuing "Assimilation"?', 241–244.

60 Adepoyibi, Adeniba C, *The Development of Responsibility and Management of Aboriginal Community Councils in East Arnhem Land and the Tiwi Islands*, Charles Darwin University (Australia), 1999, 53.

61 Oral history with authors, 30 August 2016.

62 Lovegrove to Long, 9 September 1976, NAA A2354 1982/123.

63 Walter Kerinaiua et al. to Ian Viner, 24 January 1977, NAA A2354 1982/123.

64 Eric Venbrux, 'Property Rights and Tourism in the Tiwi Islands, Northern Australia', *Property Rights & Economic Development*, 2012, 236.

65 Pirrawayingi Puruntatameri, oral history with authors, 5 September 2016.

66 Leah Kerinaiua, Tiwi principal, MSC school 2007, quoted in Frances Murray, 'The Development of Successful Bilingual, Biliterate and Bicultural Pedagogy: Place for Tiwi Teachers and Tiwi Language in Learning', in *History of Bilingual Education in the Northern Territory* (Springer, 2017), 126.

67   Teddy Portaminni, oral history with authors, 26 March 2022.

68   Teresita Puruntatameri, oral history with authors, 23 November 2015.

69   Oral history with authors, 26 September 2015.

70   Magdalen Kelantumama, oral history with authors, 28 March 2022.

71   Jane Simpson, Jo Caffery, and Patrick McConvell, *Gaps in Australia's Indigenous Language Policy: Dismantling Bilingual Education in the Northern Territory*, AIATSIS Discussion Paper Number 24, 2009, 25–26.

72   Northern Territory Emergency Response, 'Northern Territory Emergency Response: Report of the NTER Review Board', (Government of Australia, 14 October 2008), 30–31.

73   Simpson et al., *Gaps in Australia's Indigenous Language Policy*, 25–26.

74   Magdalen Kelantumama, oral history with authors, 28 March 2022.

75   Morris, 'Continuing "Assimilation"?', 238.

76   Morris, 310.

77   Pima, the Tiwi Ancestor, has also been spelled 'Bima'.

78   Eric Venbrux, 'The Post-Colonial Virtue of Aboriginal Art', *Zeitschrift Für Ethnologie*, 2002, 234.

79   Barry Puruntatameri, oral history with authors, 9 September 2016.

80   'Even a Cyclone Can't Stop the Footy', *Sydney Morning Herald*, 20 March 2005.

81   Gawin Tipiloura quoted in Peter and Sheila Forrest, *Tiwi Meet the Future: Ngawurraningimarri: All Come Together* (Winnellie, NT: Tiwi Land Council, 2005), 87.

82   Oral history with authors, 24 September 2015.

83   Teddy Portaminni, oral history with authors, 26 March 2022.

84   Elaine Tiparui, oral history with authors, 31 August 2016

85   James Darren Puantulura, oral history with authors, 24 March 2022.

86   Walter Kerinaiua Jnr, oral history with authors, 24 March 2022.

87   Frances Kerinaiua, oral history with authors, 11 June 2016.

88   Oral history with authors, 24 September 2015.

89   Magdalen Kelantumama, oral history with authors, 28 March 2022.

ACKNOWLEDGEMENTS

This book would not have been possible without the contribution of our Tiwi research partners, historians and cultural advisers. We are indebted to the staff of the Patakijiyali Museum – Fiona Kerinaiua, Ancilla Kurrupuwu and Yvette Tipumamantumiri – for their guidance and generous sharing of cultural and historical knowledge.

We are especially grateful to all those who contributed oral histories:

Agnes Kerinaiua; Ancilla Kurrupuwu; Anne Puruntatameri; Augusta Punguangi; Barbarita Timaeputua; Barry Puruntatameri; Bede Tungutalum; Bernard Tipiloura; Calista Kantilla; Consolata Kelantumama; Dulcie Kelantumama; Elaine Tiparui; Enid Cunningham; Esther Babui; Eunice Orsto; Yikiliya Eustace Tipiloura; Fiona Kerinaiua; Frances Kerinaiua; Francillia Puruntatameri; George Stassi; Henrietta Hunter; Jacinta Tipunguruti; James Darren Puantulua; Jane Alimankinni; Karen Tipiloura; Kerryanne Kerinaiua; Leonie Tipiloura; Magdalen Kelantumama; Marcella Fernando; Marie Carmel Tipurupilimau; Marie Cecile Tipiloura; Marilyn Kerinaiua; Marita Pikalui; Neville Wommatakimmi; Pirrawayingi Marius Puruntatameri; Richard Tungutalum; Romolo Kantilla; Stanley Tipungwuti; Teddy Portaminni; Teresita Kilipayu Puruntatameri; Therese Bourke; Walter Kerinaiua Jnr.

We are also grateful to Sr Anne Gardiner Punganimawu for her assistance with the historical research as well as Lane Sladovich. We also thank Stacey Parker and her family for permission to use the late Harold Porkilari's stunning artwork for our cover. Fr Pat and Sr Robyn Reynolds gave us great encouragement. Kevin Doolan provided important direction and advice. Dr Genevieve Campbell from the University of Sydney also assisted with research leads. Zoe Smith was invaluable as a research assistant and Dr Alexis Bergantz translated French sources for us.

None of this could have proceeded without the support and permission of the Tiwi Land Council, for which we are deeply grateful, as well as the support of the Tiwi Regional Shire Council and the Mantiyupwi Clan Group. Tiwi Resources provided logistical support in Wurrumiyanga (and we thank Yvonne Kelly in particular), as did Catholic Care. We are grateful to the OLSH sisters, the MSC priests and the Catholic Diocese of Darwin for sharing their historical documents. We also thank the Northern Territory Library (and Dr Charlie Ward and Helen Sartinas in particular), the National Archives in Darwin and the Northern Territory Archives Centre for their support in the documentary archives.

This project was enabled by funding from the Australian National University's Grand Challenges Scheme and the project *Beyond Reconciliation: Truth telling for Indigenous Wellbeing*. We were also supported by the University of Notre Dame's Cushwa Centre, the Australian Research in Theology Foundation, the Australian Catholic University's Golding Centre (especially the late Sr Sophie McGrath) and the Australian Research Council (grant no. DE220100042). We also wish to thank the ANU's School of History for its support and particularly Dr Lawrence Bamblett, Dr Robyn McKenzie and Prof Maria Nugent for their encouragement and leadership through the *Beyond Reconciliation* project.

Most of all, we thank the Tiwi people for sharing such rich stories of their pasts. We pay our respects to those who have been involved in the project but did not live to see it come to completion. May they rest in peace with their Ancestors. We hope that this book will be of great interest and encouragement to all Tiwi people for generations to come. Most of all, we thank the Tiwi people for sharing such rich stories of their pasts. We hope that this book will be of great interest and encouragement to you and for generations to come.